NATIONAL GEOGRAPHIC KiDS

weird but true!

Ancient Egypt

know-it-all

NATIONAL GEOGRAPHIC KiDS

weird but true!

know-it-all

Ancient Egypt

SARAH WASSNER FLYNN

ILLUSTRATED BY
SANJIDA RASHID

NATIONAL GEOGRAPHIC
WASHINGTON, D.C.

CONTENTS

ANCIENT
...AND AWESOME!

THE **OLDEST EVER** COMPLETE **MUMMY** DISCOVERED IN ANCIENT EGYPT DATES BACK **OVER 5,000 YEARS!**

THIS SARCOPHAGUS, OR COFFIN, IS JUST ONE OF MANY ARTIFACTS UNEARTHED FROM THE ANCIENT EGYPTIAN CIVILIZATION.

From pharaohs to pyramids and tombs to Tut, ancient Egypt was mystical, mysterious—and totally mind-boggling. This early civilization emerged as a powerful, advanced empire when the rest of the world was still figuring things out. And it wasn't just a passing fad: Egypt was a dominant civilization in the Mediterranean for almost 30 centuries! So just how did this hot, dry desert place come to reign supreme? The credit goes to a long line of leaders who, for the most part, ruled mightily to unify their people (sometimes against the odds!). Location didn't hurt either: The annual flooding of the Nile River transformed the Egyptian desert into fertile farmland. As a result, the Egyptians had a steady stream (eh, get it?) of food, water, and supplies right there on the banks of the river. They were so good at farming that they even had a surplus of crops and other goodies, which led to a thriving trade system. Their economy was booming, and, at one point, they were most likely the most powerful civilization in the world. In a nutshell, ancient Egypt was one happenin' hot spot.

HISTORY'S MYSTERIES

Life in ancient Egypt was chock-full of colorful culture, from advanced writing systems to incredible artwork that still exist today. But there are also hints of a bygone era: quirky customs, wacky practices (um, treating wounds with moldy bread? Gross!), even vengeful curses! How do we know? After all, pharaohs couldn't exactly post a pic with a pyramid or snap a selfie with the Sphinx. Thanks to the many artifacts the Egyptians left behind, scientists have been able to literally dig up details about their day-to-day lives. Major discoveries—including King Tut's tomb in 1922—have helped experts piece together Egypt's past. After so many years of searching and digging, it might seem that there's nowhere else to look for new artifacts. But discoveries are still being made—and scientists are applying new tech to older artifacts to uncover even more about the stuff that's already been unearthed. This means that the more technology advances, the more we'll know about ancient Egypt.

EVERYDAY PEOPLE

Ancient Egyptians ... they're just like us. Well, sort of. Sure, some of them may have made mummies out of their dead loved ones, but they also went about their daily lives a lot like we do. They had tight-knit families, went to school, held jobs, and ran businesses. They also came up with some incredible inventions that made life a lot easier for them—many of which we still use today. Of course, there were plenty of differences between life today and back then (it was thousands of years ago, after all), but the incredible thing is that they were advanced enough that we can still see some similarities today.

WHO WAS HERODOTUS?

A lot of the weirdest stuff we know about the ancient Egyptians comes from the writings of the famous Greek scholar Herodotus. He traveled to Egypt in the mid-400s B.C. and came home with wild tales of the people who lived there (things like "they knead dough with their feet" and "women make water [go to the bathroom] standing up and the men crouching down"). But experts aren't so sure if Herodotus's words were actual observations, or if the Egyptians just told him these wacky tales to have fun with the foreigner. Because of this, it's key we take the most bizarre tidbits about the Egyptians with a grain of, uh, sand.

ANCIENT EGYPT

BY THE NUMBERS

1 Number of major organs left in the body after mummification. The heart was kept inside, but all other organs were removed.

9 Age that King Tut became pharaoh of Egypt, in 1332 B.C.

97 Percentage of ancient Egyptian land that was covered in desert.

130 Number of Egyptian pyramids discovered to date.

2.8 TONS (2.5 t) Weight of a single stone block used to build a pyramid.

1 MILE (1.6 km) The average length of the bandages used on an ancient Egyptian mummy.

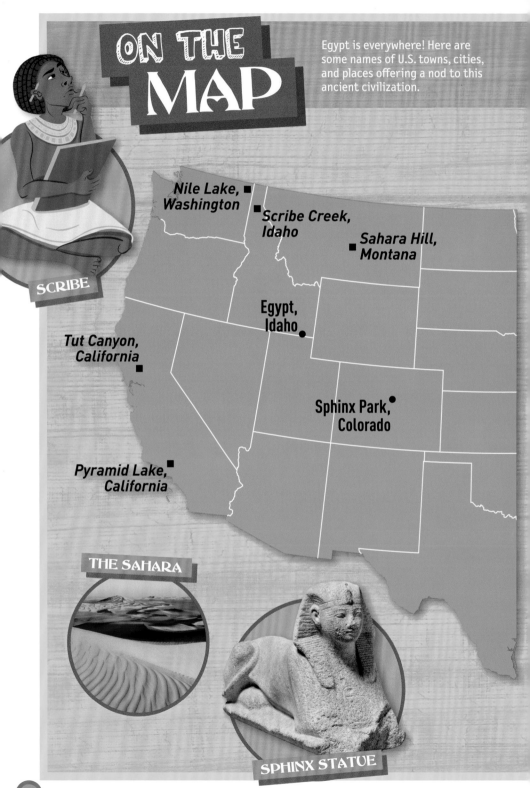

ON THE MAP

Egypt is everywhere! Here are some names of U.S. towns, cities, and places offering a nod to this ancient civilization.

SCRIBE

Nile Lake, Washington

Scribe Creek, Idaho

Sahara Hill, Montana

Egypt, Idaho

Tut Canyon, California

Sphinx Park, Colorado

Pyramid Lake, California

THE SAHARA

SPHINX STATUE

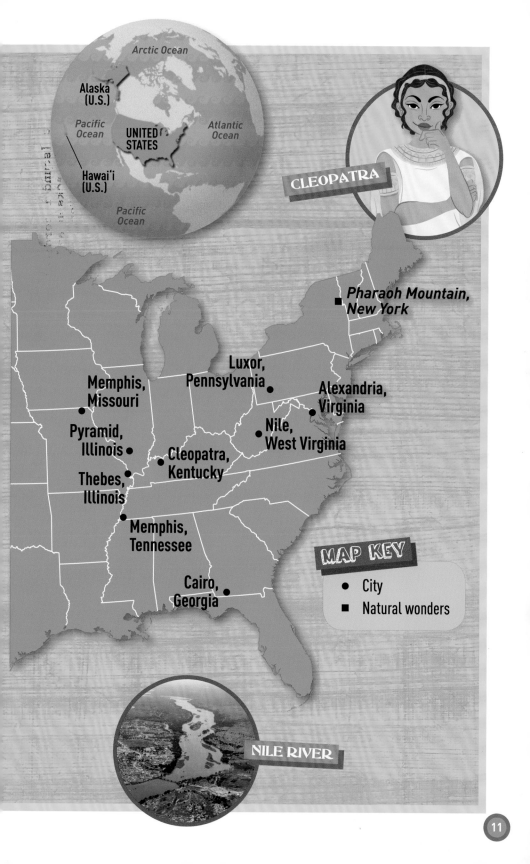

Arctic Ocean

Alaska
(U.S.)

Pacific
Ocean

UNITED
STATES

Atlantic
Ocean

Hawai'i
(U.S.)

Pacific
Ocean

CLEOPATRA

■ Pharaoh Mountain,
New York

Luxor,
Pennsylvania

Memphis,
Missouri

Alexandria,
Virginia

Pyramid,
Illinois

Nile,
West Virginia

Cleopatra,
Kentucky

Thebes,
Illinois

Memphis,
Tennessee

Cairo,
Georgia

MAP KEY

● City
■ Natural wonders

NILE RIVER

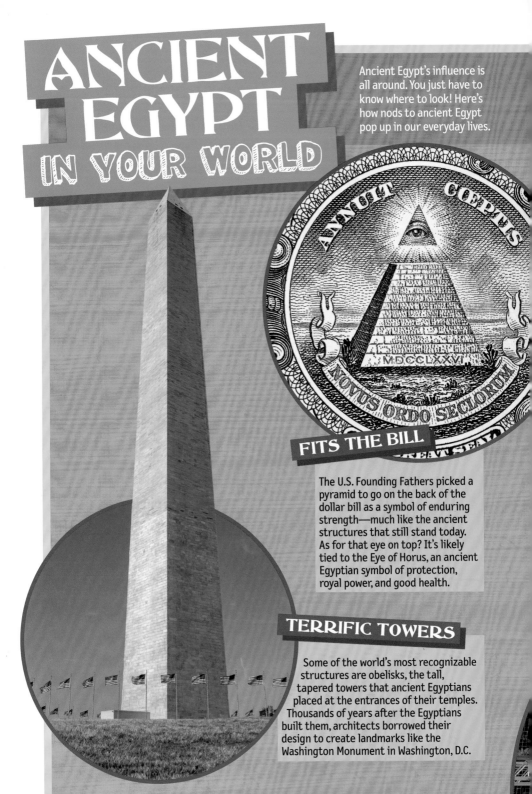

ANCIENT EGYPT IN YOUR WORLD

Ancient Egypt's influence is all around. You just have to know where to look! Here's how nods to ancient Egypt pop up in our everyday lives.

FITS THE BILL

The U.S. Founding Fathers picked a pyramid to go on the back of the dollar bill as a symbol of enduring strength—much like the ancient structures that still stand today. As for that eye on top? It's likely tied to the Eye of Horus, an ancient Egyptian symbol of protection, royal power, and good health.

TERRIFIC TOWERS

Some of the world's most recognizable structures are obelisks, the tall, tapered towers that ancient Egyptians placed at the entrances of their temples. Thousands of years after the Egyptians built them, architects borrowed their design to create landmarks like the Washington Monument in Washington, D.C.

BOOK IT

Best-selling author Rick Riordan drew on the stories of Egyptian mythology to write the Kane Chronicles. The three-book series centers on two siblings—who happen to be the descendants of pharaohs—and their adventures with ancient Egyptian gods.

PRETTY SMART

Today's makeup industry might look a lot different if it weren't for the ancient Egyptians, who introduced the use of eye makeup, lipstick, and other beauty products.

BE THEIR GUEST

Visitors who check into the pyramid-shaped Luxor Hotel & Casino in Las Vegas, Nevada, U.S.A., are greeted by a replica of the Sphinx that's even bigger than the real deal at Giza.

AN ANCIENT LAND

Where in the world was ancient Egypt? It's in the same place modern-day Egypt is today, sitting in the northeast corner of Africa. In ancient times, the Egyptian civilization was centered around the Nile River. The people set up homes and villages in the fertile river valleys and built their now famous pyramids on the west bank of the Nile.

EUROPE

ASIA

Atlantic Ocean

Egypt

AFRICA

Indian Ocean

SOUTH AMERICA

ISRAEL

JORDAN

MEDITERRANEAN SEA

Alexandria

Nile Delta

Great Pyramids and
Great Sphinx of Giza

Cairo

Pyramid of Djoser

Memphis

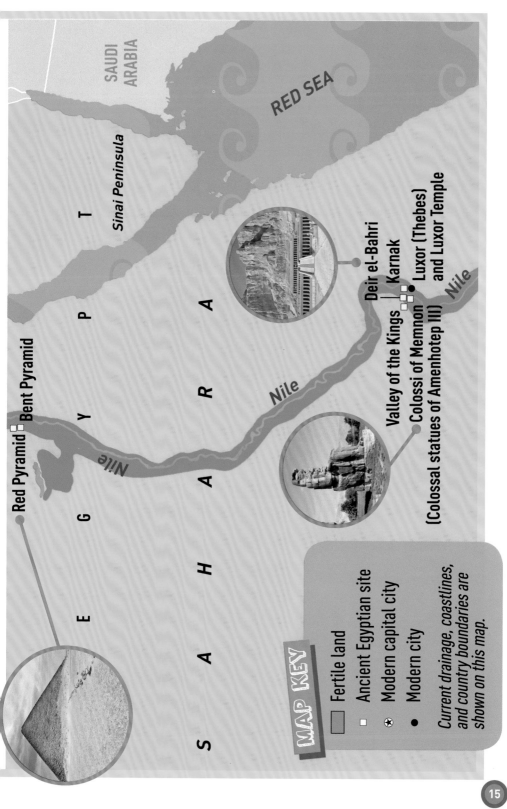

Red Pyramid   Bent Pyramid

E   G   Y   P   T

S   A   H   A   R   A

Nile

Nile

Sinai Peninsula

SAUDI
ARABIA

RED SEA

Deir el-Bahri
Valley of the Kings   Karnak
Colossi of Memnon   Luxor (Thebes)
(Colossal statues of Amenhotep III)   and Luxor Temple

Nile

MAP KEY

☐ Fertile land
■ Ancient Egyptian site
⊛ Modern capital city
● Modern city

*Current drainage, coastlines,
and country boundaries are
shown on this map.*

15

Ancient Egypt
Through the Years

The ancient Egyptian civilization is divided into time spans called periods and kingdoms. Sometimes after a kingdom there was an intermediate period, in-between times usually marked by chaos and unrest due to the lack of a strong ruling family. Here's a look at some highlights—and lowlights— through the years.

① PREHISTORIC PERIOD

7000–5000 B.C.
Tribes of hunters and gatherers live scattered around the Nile River.

1. PREHISTORIC PERIOD	2. PREDYNASTIC PERIOD

7000 B.C.	6000 B.C.	5000 B.C.	4000 B.C.

② PREDYNASTIC PERIOD

5000–2950 B.C.
Ancient Egypt thrives! Religion, kingship, and art begin to take shape.

③ EARLY DYNASTIC PERIOD

2950–2575 B.C.
King Menes unites Egypt.

Hieroglyphs are invented.

④ OLD KINGDOM

2575–2125 B.C.

The Great Pyramid as we know it is built.

The art of mummification begins.

⑤ FIRST INTERMEDIATE PERIOD

2125–2010 B.C.

Rival kings squabble, causing the Two Lands to splinter.

⑥ MIDDLE KINGDOM

2010–1630 B.C.

Egypt is reunited once more.

Its borders expand into the gold-rich land of Nubia.

---

3. EARLY DYNASTIC PERIOD	4. OLD KINGDOM	5. FIRST INTERMEDIATE PERIOD	6. MIDDLE KINGDOM	7. SECOND INTERMEDIATE PERIOD	8. NEW KINGDOM	9. END OF ANCIENT EGYPT

3000 B.C.   **2000 B.C.**   **1000 B.C.**   **0 B.C.**

---

⑦ SECOND INTERMEDIATE PERIOD

1630–1539 B.C.

It's war! Foreign settlers take control of Lower Egypt (they're eventually driven out).

⑧ NEW KINGDOM

1539–1069 B.C.

Famous pharaohs (like King Tut) rule!

Egypt gets richer and more powerful than ever.

⑨ THE END OF ANCIENT EGYPT

1069–30 B.C.

Egypt is invaded, and foreign leaders take over for centuries.

Some ancient traditions are maintained, but Egypt will not be fully independent for another 2,300 years.

LUSH LIFE

Some 8,000 years ago, long before the ancient Egyptian civilization started, the region was a totally different place. It was a vast grassland where early humans likely flocked to the banks of the Nile to hunt, gather, and fish, and eventually established homes around the river.

A SUDDEN CHANGE

So how did this area go from grassland to desert? Around 5000 B.C., a dramatic shift occurred in Earth's climate. Scientists aren't sure what exactly caused it, although some theorize that it had to do with a change in weather patterns or Earth's orbit, which may have increased the amount of sun the area received. Other experts think that nomads had something to do with it, since their goats may have overgrazed the grasses, which led to a reduction of moisture in the air and dried up the atmosphere. Whatever the reason, Earth warmed up and most of the grasslands in Egypt slowly turned into a desert over the course of about 1,000 years.

Don't blame me!

ANIMAL **BONES** FOUND IN THE **SAHARAN SANDS** SHOW THAT **GIRAFFES AND ELEPHANTS** ONCE ROAMED AROUND WHAT IS NOW A VAST, DRY DESERT.

SETTLING IN

With their grasslands drying up, the native Egyptian people adapted. If the water wouldn't come to them, they would go to the water! That meant settling around the Nile River. Since rainfall had become less frequent and less reliable, they set up farming communities, growing wheat and flax. They wove linen fabrics and produced pottery. They even traded with other nearby civilizations and acquired coveted commodities like turquoise and wood, which they used to make jewelry and tools, among other items essential to daily life. As farmers, they stayed put to tend to their crops and animals, giving up their nomadic lifestyle. Settling in the area surrounding the Nile River resulted in the development of small but distinct kingdoms, sparking the very early beginnings of human civilization and culture.

Born to be wild

CAMELS WERE DOMESTI- CATED MORE THAN **3,000** YEARS AGO.

ANCIENT WALL PAINTINGS SHOW EGYPTIAN FARMERS TENDING THEIR CROPS.

COMING TOGETHER

The earliest days of Egypt are known as the pre-dynastic period, before any kings came forward to unify the land. It's even before the pyramids were built. Yep, a very long time ago! Order among the small kingdoms was upheld by tribal chiefs and kings, who, as time went on, bonded together (or conquered one another) to create bigger kingdoms. Eventually, the land was parceled off into just two large kingdoms: one where the Nile River enters the Mediterranean Sea, and the other to the south. Despite sharing so much of the same background and culture, the two kingdoms were at odds with each other. It took multiple attempts by incoming kings (and hundreds of years) to bring the two sides together and squash their squabbling for good.

RAIN, RAIN, GO AWAY

Grasslands drying up into a desert certainly isn't something you see every day. Or every millennia, for that matter. Scientists say that what happened on Earth to make the Sahara go from green to brown likely occurs about every 30,000 years! Now, after thousands of years of less rain and more sun, a once lush land has been transformed into one of the driest places on the planet. Today, on average, only an inch (2.5 cm) of rain falls in Egypt each year.

The Gift of the Nile

The River That GAVE THE EGYPTIANS LIFE

AT OVER **4,100 MILES** (6,598 KM) LONG, THE **NILE RIVER** IS THE **LONGEST RIVER** IN THE **WORLD.**

FLOODING IN

When is a flood a good thing? When it means that flood water saturates otherwise dry-as-a-bone soil and makes the land go from barren to bountiful! This is what happened on the Nile River in ancient times every year around June, when melting snowfall and heavy rains from the Ethiopian Highlands south of Egypt caused the river to burst beyond its banks. The result: When the water eventually receded, or went back to its normal levels, it left behind a layer of rich, dense soil, also known as silt. More fertile than other types of soil, silt is able to retain water and promotes air circulation, which helps crops grow. So, with a valley full of fertile soil, the desert was transformed into a desirable place to live.

A SECRET TO SURVIVAL

The flooding—which typically lasted from June to October—became the ancient Egyptian civilization's secret to survival. The river allowed Egyptians to trade and travel from place to place, and gave them access to important resources like papyrus reeds, which grew along its banks. So it's no wonder that Greek historian Herodotus called Egypt "the gift of the Nile." The country truly couldn't exist without this river.

REED ALL ABOUT IT

Deserts aren't necessarily known for their forests, which made wood and timber hard to come by for the ancient Egyptians. So they reached for another woodlike resource instead: papyrus. This hollow reed popped up in the marshes and swamps near the river, and the Egyptians used every part of it. They bundled them up to build small fishing boats, and turned them into sandals, ropes, baskets, and other everyday items. They also removed the plant's fiber and mashed it up to create a flat material they could write on—something similar to what we know now as *paper* (get it?).

ROLLING ON A RIVER

Being near the Nile River meant the Egyptians could truly go places! Picture it as a highway on water, with boats sailing up and down the river. Wealthy families would take long trips on luxurious boats, fishermen would sail on smaller vessels, and builders piled large stone blocks and other heavy material into boats to take to new temple sites via the river. And because the Nile was the quickest and easiest way to travel from place to place, its waters provided a streamlined channel for trade between Egypt and other civilizations. This helped boost Egypt's economy and extend its power among other countries.

5 FLOWING FACTS ABOUT THE NILE RIVER

1. Today, the Nile flows through 11 countries. They are South Sudan, Sudan, Uganda, Rwanda, Burundi, the Democratic Republic of the Congo, Tanzania, Kenya, Ethiopia, Eritrea, and Egypt.

2. The Nile is home to the Blue Nile waterfall, which is nearly the same height as Niagara Falls.

3. The ancient Egyptians believed that the floodwaters were the tears of a goddess.

4. A man once spent nine months walking the entire length of the Nile.

5. Some 95 percent of all Egyptians today live within 12 miles (19 km) of the Nile River.

Onward!

A MODEL OF AN ANCIENT PADDLING BOAT, USED TO NAVIGATE THE NILE RIVER

Grow On!
PLANNING AND PLANTING
Around the Nile's Annual Flood

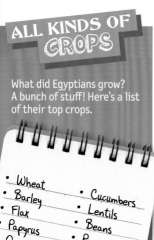

ALL KINDS OF CROPS

What did Egyptians grow? A bunch of stuff! Here's a list of their top crops.

- Wheat
- Barley
- Flax
- Papyrus
- Onions
- Garlic
- Leeks
- Radishes
- Lettuce
- Cucumbers
- Lentils
- Beans
- Pomegranates
- Vines
- Figs
- Dates
- Grapes
- Melons

DOWN ON THE FARM

Ancient Egyptian farmers really relied on the river. They built their lives around the rise and fall of the Nile's waters and even created seasons based on where the water stood. Because sciences like meteorology and biology were not around (or understood) just yet, the Egyptians credited the flood—also known as the inundation—to the gods. They even held an annual festival to celebrate the goddess Isis, since they thought her tears (not the melting snow in the mountains of southern Africa) made the Nile overflow each year.

COOL TOOL

Usually the Nile's floods were fabulous for Egyptians. But sometimes the floods were lower than expected, which led to drought and famine, or too high, which could sweep away homes and ruin crops. So the Egyptians came up with a handy tool called a nilometer to measure floodwaters. This circular well—about as wide as a garage door and made from large limestone blocks—was connected to the Nile through an underground channel. The river water would rush in, and Egyptians were able to measure the height of the Nile by looking at markings they had made on the inside wall of the well. Taking note of either extremely high or low water levels then helped farmers prepare for a less-than-healthy harvest.

'Tis the Season

Egyptian farmers divided the year into three seasons: the flooding season, the growing season, and the harvesting season.

AKHET

ALSO KNOWN AS: Flood

WHEN: Mid-June to mid-October

The farmers couldn't do much with their land while it was underwater, so they spent the off-season working as laborers on construction sites for pyramids and other big buildings.

PERET

ALSO KNOWN AS: Growth

WHEN: Mid-October to mid-February

As soon as the land started emerging from the flood, the farmers got to work. They'd plant seeds for crops and use animals to trample seeds into the ground.

SHEMU

ALSO KNOWN AS: Harvest

WHEN: Mid-February to mid-June

As the crops popped up in the late spring, the farmers gathered all of the goods—and collected seeds for the following year's growth season.

THE ANCIENT EGYPTIANS **TRAINED BABOONS** TO **PICK FRUIT** FROM **TREES.**

Outta my way!

SOME **HIPPOS** CAN **OUTRUN** A HUMAN.

HOLD BACK THE RIVER

Does the Nile still flood? Not since 1970, when the construction of the Aswan Dam curbed the annual overflow of the great river. This massive dam—which is taller than the Statue of Liberty—is considered one of the world's largest and took 10 years and more than one billion dollars to construct. One more *hard* fact about the Aswan Dam? It was made with enough rock to build 17 Great Pyramids!

WHAT LURKS BENEATH

Hippos and crocodiles, oh my! Back in ancient times, the Nile River's banks were crawling with fierce creatures—and the Egyptians lived in fear of them. Hippos were known to bump into boats and even turn them over, while crocodiles could take down anyone walking by the river's banks. As a result, the Egyptians created weapons to hunt these ferocious predators, and they also turned to the gods to ease their anxiety and protect them from these beasts.

DIG IT! When herding animals across flooded areas, the Egyptians chanted spells to drive away crocodiles.

SOMETHING FISHY

The Nile River was chock-full of fish. And the Egyptians perfected the art of fishing just like they did farming, learning how to use spears and nets made from papyrus reeds and twine to catch little swimmers under the surface. But there was one fish they always threw back into the river—the medjed. These medium-size fish were said to have taken on sacred qualities after eating part of the body of Osiris, the god of the afterlife, when he was thrown into the river by his brother. So for some Egyptians, eating the medjed would mean upsetting the gods—and bring nothing but bad luck.

DIG IT!

Modern medjed are known as elephant fish because of their long trunk-like nose.

Gods of the Nile

Egyptian religion was polytheistic—meaning they believed in many gods, or deities, who were thought to be in control of everything that happened in the world. Some gods were specifically linked to the Nile River, and the ancient Egyptians would toss gifts into the river in the hope that their gods would flood the desert. In fact, a number of monuments and sacred temples have been found close to shore. Here's a look at some of the gods who ruled the river. (To find out about many more gods that influenced other aspects of ancient Egyptian life, flip to page 102.)

TAWERET

ALSO KNOWN AS: The hippo goddess of the Nile and goddess of childbirth and pregnancy

WHY SHE WAS WORSHIPPED: She protected pregnant women and is also linked to the Nile's annual flood.

ODD DEITY DETAILS: In ancient art, Taweret is shown as a pregnant hippo with the legs of a lion and a crocodile's tail.

HAPI

ALSO KNOWN AS: God of annual flooding

WHY HE WAS WORSHIPPED: He was responsible for causing the Nile to flood each year.

ODD DEITY DETAILS: Hapi is often shown in Egyptian art as a man with a papyrus plant sprouting from the top of his head.

SOBEK

ALSO KNOWN AS: Protector against river dangers

WHY HE WAS WORSHIPPED: He controlled the fertility of the soil and also protected Egypt's armies.

ODD DEITY DETAILS: Egyptians believed that the Nile River was created from his sweat.

KHNUM

ALSO KNOWN AS: God of fertility and water

WHY HE WAS WORSHIPPED: He controlled the flow of the Nile River and made sure the right amount of silt was released into the water of the annual flood.

ODD DEITY DETAILS: Khnum is also credited with crafting humans out of clay.

SOME **300 MUMMIFIED CROCO-DILES** HAVE BEEN DISCOVERED AT ONE ANCIENT **EGYPTIAN CEMETERY** SITE TO HONOR THE **CROCODILE GOD, SOBEK.**

A Tale of Two Lands

Unification of Egypt and the
START OF THE ANCIENT CIVILIZATION

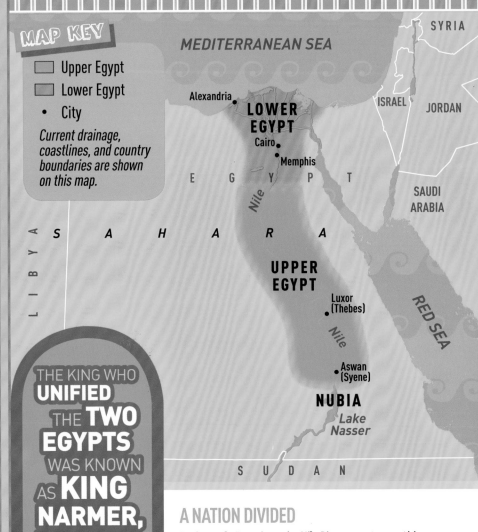

MAP KEY

- ☐ Upper Egypt
- ▨ Lower Egypt
- • City

Current drainage, coastlines, and country boundaries are shown on this map.

MEDITERRANEAN SEA

SYRIA

Alexandria

LOWER EGYPT

ISRAEL   JORDAN

Cairo

Memphis

E G Y P T

SAUDI ARABIA

Nile

S A H A R A

LIBYA

UPPER EGYPT

Luxor (Thebes)

RED SEA

Nile

Aswan (Syene)

NUBIA

Lake Nasser

S U D A N

THE KING WHO **UNIFIED** THE **TWO EGYPTS** WAS KNOWN AS **KING NARMER,** WHOSE NAME MEANT **"STRIKING CATFISH."**

A NATION DIVIDED

To the early Egyptians, the Nile River meant everything: They could farm on its fertile banks and set up shelter, and they worshipped gods by its banks. So it comes as no surprise that all Egyptian people wanted to live near it. But with so many scattered tribes living along the Nile, the land lacked a sense of community. In fact, Egypt was eventually composed of two separate, constantly clashing kingdoms: Upper Egypt and Lower Egypt.

THIS END UP?

Here's the tricky thing about early Egypt. Not only were there two Egypts at the time, but their names were totally confusing. You see, Upper Egypt actually covered the southern part of the country, while Lower Egypt claimed the northern half. Why? It has to do with Egypt's elevation—and the flow of the Nile River. Since Lower Egypt is closer to sea level, it was the lower ground. And because Upper Egypt was made up of hillier land, it got the, uh, upper hand. Also, the Nile River flows from south to north, making things even more topsy-turvy. So, without GPS satellites and modern maps, this flipped distinction made perfect sense to the Egyptians.

SEEING BLACK AND RED

To make this a little more confusing, the ancient Egyptians had their own names for their lands. Instead of using "Upper Egypt" and "Lower Egypt" (which are names that came later), back then, they divided the land based on the color of its terrain. One part was called *Kemet*, or Black Land, for its abundance of dark, fertile soil on the banks of the Nile. As for the flat, sunbaked desert? The Egyptians referred to that as the *desheret*, or "red land."

ALONG CAME A SCORPION

In Egypt's earliest days, it took two kings—and 100 years—to create one civilization out of a divided land. Researchers think the first attempt at unifying Upper and Lower Egypt was made by a king named Scorpion. How'd he get such a killer name? It comes from the image of the critter etched into a stone tablet that's thought to tell the tale of his attempted takeover. As a king from Upper Egypt, Scorpion tried to conquer the lower half around 3200 B.C. While there are no definitive details proving that Scorpion actually carried this plan to the end, experts credit him with starting the push toward unifying all of Egypt.

MENES MEANS BUSINESS

About 100 years after Scorpion, King Menes, also known as Narmer, stormed in from the south. He brought Egypt together under his rule around the year 2925 B.C. and became its first king. Menes's secret to success? Showing allegiance to both the north and south parts of Egypt by wearing a crown of two colors, representing loyalty to both lands. Menes founded Memphis, the ancient capital city, and began to oversee the beginning of the Egyptian civilization.

Much of what we know about the unification of ancient Egypt comes from discoveries made some 120 years ago in the city of Hierakonpolis. During that time, both a 5,000-year-old tablet and tomb were found in nearly perfect condition. The tablet, known as the Narmer Palette, is considered among the oldest historical documents in the world. It shows a ruler—believed to be Narmer, who also went by Menes—triumphant over his enemies, wearing the crowns of both Upper and Lower Egypt. The tomb is thought to be King Scorpion's, as indicated by hieroglyphs and rock art that show a man conquering another man wearing the symbol of Lower Egypt. Both of these ancient artifacts have helped experts piece together a better picture of the very early days of the Egyptian civilization.

The New Kingdom

How the Unification of Egypt Led to
ONE OF THE WORLD'S STRONGEST NATIONS

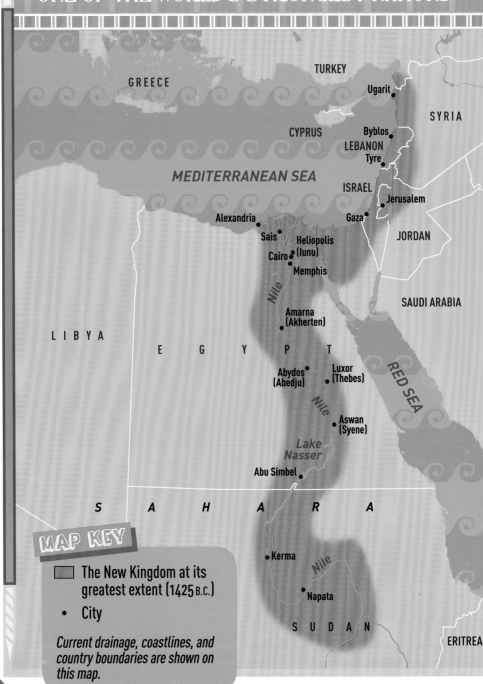

TURKEY

GREECE

Ugarit

SYRIA

CYPRUS

Byblos

LEBANON

Tyre

MEDITERRANEAN SEA

ISRAEL

Jerusalem

Alexandria

Gaza

Sais

JORDAN

Heliopolis
(Iunu)

Cairo

Memphis

SAUDI ARABIA

Nile

Amarna
(Akherten)

L I B Y A

E   G   Y   P   T

Abydos
(Abedju)

Luxor
(Thebes)

RED SEA

Nile

Aswan
(Syene)

Lake
Nasser

Abu Simbel

S   A   H   A   R   A

Kerma

Nile

Napata

S U D A N

ERITREA

MAP KEY

▢ The New Kingdom at its
greatest extent (1425 B.C.)

• City

*Current drainage, coastlines, and
country boundaries are shown on
this map.*

POWER PLAY

After King Menes unified ancient Egypt, the country steadily increased its power. Eventually, during the New Kingdom, also known as the Egyptian Empire, the civilization soared. Egypt had a booming economy, built huge temples (like the famous Luxor Temple; its ruins still stand today), and had fabulous farming, and its people were dripping with creativity. With famous pharaohs and a dominant military leading the charge, the empire expanded, stretching from ancient Syria in the northeast down to Nubia in the south.

DYNAMIC DYNASTIES

Throughout much of the ancient Egyptian civilization, the power to rule was passed from one dynasty—a big family group—to another. Each dynasty controlled the land and worked to protect and expand Egypt. And each family would stay in power until it was overthrown or out of heirs. At the top of the dynasty? The pharaoh, who was thought to be a living god. The pharaoh made up all the rules and could do just about anything he— or she—wanted to do, usually while being fanned with ostrich feathers by servants. (Turn to page 44 for more reasons why it was good to be pharaoh!)

"PHARAOH" COMES FROM THE EGYPTIAN PHRASE **MEANING "GREAT HOUSE,"** REFERRING TO THE **ROYAL PALACE.**

Power Plays
Groups That Attempted to TAKE OVER ANCIENT EGYPT

Egypt had it pretty good during the New Kingdom. But that's not to say this time was without conflict. The more lands Egypt conquered, the more enemies it made. Eventually, Egypt fought one too many battles, and the mighty empire weakened into a mere shadow of what it once was. Still, the ancient Egyptians had it made in the (palm tree) shade for many, many years. Here's a look at some of the major players who popped up while Egypt was at its pinnacle of power.

THE HYKSOS

WHAT: Nomadic people who ruled a large part of Egypt until they were forced out around 1539 B.C., sparking the start of the New Kingdom.

CLAIM TO FAME: During their reign, the Hyksos used technology to create tools and weapons out of bronze, and develop new farming methods, all of which the Egyptians eventually adopted. They also introduced the horse and chariot to Egypt.

We wouldn't have pomegranates or olives if it weren't for the Hyksos, who used their advanced farming methods to create new fruits and vegetables.

THE HITTITES

WHAT: A civilization that clashed with the ancient Egyptians over control of trade routes, as well as the city of Kadesh, which sat at the border between the two empires.

CLAIM TO FAME: Eventually, the bitter enemies came to a truce and signed the world's first peace treaty, etched on a silver tablet.

The battle between the ancient Egyptians and the Hittites is said to be one of the biggest chariot battles ever fought, with a total of some 5,000 horse-drawn chariots involved on either side.

THE NUBIANS

WHAT: People who lived along the Nile River and were part of a colony of Egypt's for more than 500 years.

CLAIM TO FAME: Home to heaps of gold ("Nubia" is linked to the Egyptian word for the valuable mineral), which gave Egypt great wealth during the New Kingdom. And, after being under a pharaohs' thumb for five centuries, the Nubians—also known as the Kushites—later conquered and ruled Egypt for almost 100 years.

After conquering Egypt, the Nubians adopted most of the country's customs, including writing with hieroglyphs, and even built their own fields of pyramids.

A GOLDEN OPPORTUNITY

Power and wealth: That's what Egypt was all about during the New Kingdom. So how did Egyptians get rich? Here's a hint: It's shiny, it's yellow, and it's found underground. That's right, gold! Once the Egyptians expanded into Nubia, they were able to tap into the region's many mines and unearth oodles of the valuable mineral. They traded and bartered with it and used it to fashion everything from hats to shoes to jewelry. They even buried the dead with gobs of gold. While much of the era's precious metal was stolen or melted down long ago, some artifacts remain from as far back as 4,000 years ago. Now that's some old gold.

Society Rules

Ancient Egypt's SOCIAL STRUCTURE

If it isn't broken, why fix it? That was pretty much the motto of the ancient Egyptians, who kept the same setup in their society for thousands of years. From priests to policemen, almost everyone had a job to do. Here's how this civilization's social structure worked, from top to bottom.

PHARAOH

VIZIER

NOMARCHS, PRIESTS, AND PRIESTESSES

SOLDIERS

SCRIBES

MERCHANTS

CRAFTSPERSON

FARMERS

SERVANTS

THE PHARAOH

People believed pharaohs to be living gods.

THE TASKS: Ruling the land and overseeing the army.

A powerful king, the pharaoh was at the top of the pyramid. This rich and powerful leader was in charge of maintaining order, or balance, throughout the land.

VIZIER

THE TASKS: Advising the pharaoh and overseeing the government.

As the pharaoh's chief adviser, the vizier was his or her right-hand man—or woman. The vizier visited the palace daily for face time with the pharaoh to offer updates on the latest news around town. The vizier was also in charge of every aspect of Egypt's government, from farming to finance. To be a top-notch vizier (and deal with sometimes fussy pharaohs), the ideal candidate had to be smart, loyal, and levelheaded.

Every day, the vizier wrote a report on what was going on all over Egypt to give to the pharaoh.

PRIESTS AND PRIESTESSES

THE TASKS: Taking care of temples dedicated to the gods.

The ancient Egyptians feared that upsetting the gods could bring catastrophes, like drought and famine, so the priests were tasked with appeasing these mythical masters through special ceremonies at their temples. After all, if the gods weren't happy, no one was happy!

Some priests wore a leopard-skin pelt over their clothes.

NOMARCHS

THE TASKS: Governing smaller regions and making local laws.

These lawmakers ruled over regions within Egypt, known as nomes, like a mayor or governor does today. Appointed by the pharaoh, the leaders—also known as nomarchs—were trusted to oversee major projects like building irrigation canals and dams.

Each nomarch had his own local army.

SCRIBES

THE TASKS: Jotting down everything to do with daily life.

The ancient Egyptians were totally into record-keeping. And scribes were the smarties who took notes on everything from the amount of crops a harvest yielded to how many gifts a certain god received. They also kept government records for the vizier. In fact, a lot of what we now know about this time comes from scribes' detailed notes. Good thing they paid attention!

Among ancient Egyptians, just two out of 100 people could read and write.

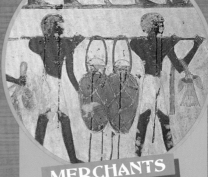

SOLDIERS

THE TASKS: Protecting the land against enemies.

This crew was Egypt's first line of defense for every battle. The army included both foot soldiers, who fought on the ground, and charioteers, who fought from horse-drawn chariots.

Some soldiers were given gold jewelry for their service.

MERCHANTS

THE TASKS: Trading goods with other countries and within Egypt.

Bounty from the harvest, specifically grain, was a hot commodity to other countries that didn't have Egypt's agricultural luck. So merchants would travel up and down the Nile to other lands to sell grain, plus other goods like gold, papyrus, and linen, in exchange for things like copper, iron, ivory, and precious stones.

Some merchants brought animals like baboons and lions from other countries to live on palace or temple grounds.

CRAFTSPERSON

THE TASKS: Making goods for the Egyptian traders who traveled up and down the Nile River.

This creative crew made everything from beads to bowls. Throughout ancient Egypt, you could find workshops where the craftspeople would gather to paint, weave, sew, or whittle—the goods eventually being sold or traded to keep Egypt's economy booming.

Most artists didn't sign their work or show any ownership of it.

FARMERS

THE TASKS: Growing food, tending to fields, raising animals, and more.

Farmers, who made up about 80 percent of Egyptian society, didn't just grow crops and feed animals. They were also expected to work in stone quarries and build pyramids and other temples during the off-season.

Farmers accepted payment in grain, not currency.

SERVANTS

THE TASKS: Working in the fields and being domestic servants for wealthy Egyptians.

Hardworking and faithful, servants often worked in the homes of pharaohs, nobles, and priests. Others worked in mines, quarries, and fields doing manual labor, like building roads.

To avoid more backbreaking work, some people actually paid to be servants in the Egyptian temples.

KEEPING THE STATUS QUO

Moving on up? Not always. In ancient Egypt, your status was usually based on your relationship to the pharaoh. He or she would often appoint sons (and, sometimes, daughters) to the top roles. But that's not to say no one was ever able to climb the social ladder. A farmer's son, for example, could go to school to learn how to be an artisan or a merchant, or even a scribe. Having desirable traits like being able to read and write or studying a specific trade in school could quite possibly score you a coveted job, no matter who you were related to.

Odd Jobs
Wacky Ways Some Egyptians EARNED A LIVING

WORKING FOR IT

Sure, there were lots of rich people like pharaohs and nobles living the golden life in ancient Egypt. But most of the civilization consisted of a middle class who held steady jobs. Back then, the jobs were a bit different than what we see today. First off, instead of a five-day week, people would work nine days in a row with just one day off in between. And they wouldn't make actual money, since coins and other forms of currency didn't enter the picture until the Persians invaded Egypt around 500 B.C. Instead, they'd get paid in goods like grain, linen, and oil. Many workers also earned benefits like paid sick days and free doctor's visits. Not too shabby!

You Do What?

So what did people do all day? Most of the career force was made up of normal gigs, like soldiers, farmers, and craftsmen. A small percentage of people worked as scribes, and other educated Egyptians went on to top jobs like viziers, priests, and architects, who designed palaces, temples, and tombs. But there were other ways to make a living. Here's a rundown of some of the weirder jobs of ancient Egypt.

SCORPION CHARMER

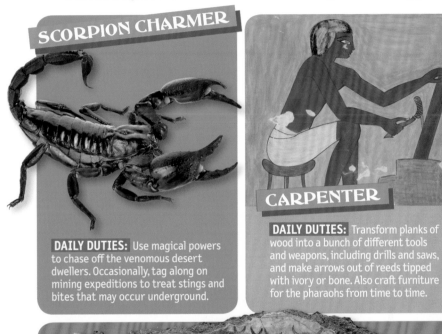

DAILY DUTIES: Use magical powers to chase off the venomous desert dwellers. Occasionally, tag along on mining expeditions to treat stings and bites that may occur underground.

CARPENTER

DAILY DUTIES: Transform planks of wood into a bunch of different tools and weapons, including drills and saws, and make arrows out of reeds tipped with ivory or bone. Also craft furniture for the pharaohs from time to time.

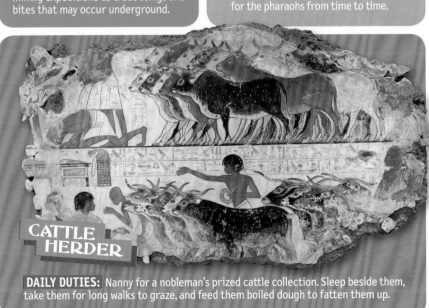

CATTLE HERDER

DAILY DUTIES: Nanny for a nobleman's prized cattle collection. Sleep beside them, take them for long walks to graze, and feed them boiled dough to fatten them up.

METALWORKER

DAILY DUTIES: Work with a fiery furnace to melt down copper, gold, and silver and pour the molten metals into molds to create sturdy weapons and jewelry.

BUTCHER

DAILY DUTIES: Cut cattle and oxen meat and sell it to Egypt's upper class (many large estates in ancient Egypt included a butcher shop).

FISHERMAN

DAILY DUTIES: Sail the Nile to catch fish using nets and harpoons, and sometimes by tying fishing line to a finger and reeling them in that way. Occasionally, "water jousting" with rival fishing boats trying to overtake territory, using large poles to try to knock the competing fishermen into the Nile.

DOCTOR

DAILY DUTIES: Take care of patients' ailments and injuries in a bunch of unusual ways, like spreading animal poop on wounds to help them heal faster (turn to page 156 for more bizarre medical treatments of the time).

POLICE OFFICER

DAILY DUTIES: Keep the peace on the streets by guarding public places like markets, temples, and parks. Protect yourself with a shield and sharp arrows, and train dogs and monkeys to help you fight crime.

DIG IT! Ancient Egyptians formed the world's first police force.

MANUAL LABORER

DAILY DUTIES: Hoist heavy rocks, lay bricks, mix mortar, and do other odd jobs that contribute to the construction of tombs and temples—sometimes completely naked if it gets too hot in the desert sun.

Far-Out Pharaohs
Kings and Queens Who MADE THEIR MARK

PART OF THE TEMPLE OF QUEEN HATSHEPSUT, THE FIRST KNOWN FEMALE PHARAOH

LUCKY LEADERS

A gorgeous home, adoring fans, unlimited power—in ancient Egypt, being a pharaoh had its perks! Treated like rock stars, they hardly had to lift a finger. And why would they? There was a staff of hundreds to cater to their every need. Pharaohs weren't just mighty leaders: The Egyptians also believed they had some kind of influence in controlling the weather, the Nile floodwaters, and the growth of crops. Simply put, they were seen as the closest living beings to the gods.

PASS THE CROWN DOWN

A pharaoh typically got to the throne simply by being born into the right family. The crown was usually passed down from one heir to another within the royal family—or dynasty—with some exceptions, like Amenemhet I, who became pharaoh after being born a commoner. Princes would be groomed from birth to be king one day. They'd train all day to become strong and quick while learning skills like taming wild horses, fishing, hunting, and military tactics.

(SOME) WOMEN RULED, TOO

And if there wasn't a direct heir? The crown would then go to a close relative or, sometimes, the pharaoh's wife. Records show that there were at least seven female pharaohs throughout ancient Egyptian civilization. But these ladies weren't called queens back then. That wasn't a word used in the ancient Egyptian language, so rulers were known as pharaohs, whether they were women or men.

5 FANTASTIC FACTS
ABOUT PHARAOHS

1. To prove his or her fitness to hold the throne, a pharaoh had to run timed laps around a track every 30 years.

2. Ancient Egyptians buried their pharaohs with many of their belongings to ensure a happy afterlife.

3. A pharaoh's *nemes*—the striped head cloth covering the head and neck—may have been worn to mimic a lion's mane.

4. Many pharaohs wore fake beards, possibly to look like the god Osiris.

5. The youngest known pharaoh was six years old. And he ruled until he was 100!

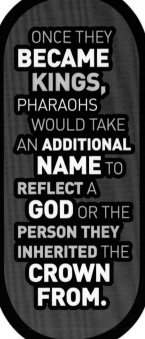

ONCE THEY **BECAME KINGS,** PHARAOHS WOULD TAKE AN **ADDITIONAL NAME** TO **REFLECT** A **GOD** OR THE **PERSON THEY INHERITED** THE **CROWN FROM.**

A PHARAOH'S TO-DOS

☐ Please the gods.

☐ Keep Egypt safe.

☐ Increase the size of the country by conquering neighboring people.

☐ Build tombs and statues. The bigger the better!

Khufu
The Pharaoh Who Built the
GREAT PYRAMID AT GIZA

A GREAT LEGACY

Little is known about this early leader, other than one lasting legacy: the Great Pyramid at Giza. Some 4,500 years ago, Khufu oversaw the construction of this tomb and monument—whose base spreads across a space wider than 13 soccer fields and originally towered 479 feet (146 m) tall—which he deemed to be his final resting spot. Ancient texts written about the king suggest that Khufu was a tyrant who cared little about Egypt's economy—he wanted all of the resources to go to his pyramid.

These stories may be the stuff of myth, but it's pretty clear that Khufu was, in fact, a single-minded monarch. After all, the construction of the pyramid took some 23 years—the same length of time that Khufu ruled. So, researchers think he spent his whole reign working on it. Today, 4,500 years later, his Great Pyramid is the only original ancient wonder of the world that's still standing.

SUCH A SHOW-OFF

Pyramids weren't cheap! But cost was no object for leaders like Khufu. At the time of his reign, Egypt was dripping in riches, thanks to trade and a thriving farming system. Experts think that Khufu wanted to flaunt that wealth—and satisfy his mega ego—with his massive monument. And that he did: Scientists say that, based on the materials used and the labor that went into constructing the Great Pyramid at Giza, the project would cost the equivalent of $5 billion in today's money. That's one pricey pyramid.

PIECES OF THE PAST!
NEW SCANS OF OLD STUFF

While the spirit of Khufu still looms large over Egypt, his physical remains disappeared long ago—likely at the hands of tomb robbers. But the search for clues about Khufu continues. A crew recently used high-powered scanning technology to reveal a 100-foot (30.5-m)-long empty space inside the Great Pyramid, close to the chambers where Khufu and his wife were buried. They haven't figured out just what the chamber was used for, but the discovery underlined that as technology continues to advance, there may be much more to learn about this elusive pharaoh—and the ancient wonder he left behind.

DIG IT!

Khufu was buried with many items, including a 50-foot (15-m) boat disassembled into 1,224 pieces.

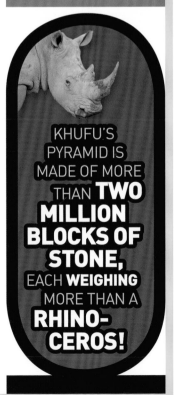

KHUFU'S PYRAMID IS MADE OF MORE THAN **TWO MILLION BLOCKS OF STONE,** EACH **WEIGHING** MORE THAN A **RHINO-CEROS!**

Senwosret III
The Pharaoh Who Extended
EGYPT'S BORDERS

BUILDING A STRONGER EGYPT

Senwosret III may come across as grumpy in ancient art, but the truth is, he had plenty to smile about. Among his many accomplishments? Completely reshaping Egypt's government. When Senwosret III came to power, Egypt's central government was very weak. The country was divvied up among many nomarchs, or regional governors, who each had control over their own districts. Ever hear the phrase "too many cooks in the kitchen"? Well, that's what Egypt was like. With so many regional leaders doing their own thing, Senwosret III sensed he wouldn't be able to maintain *Maat*—or harmony and balance—he needed to keep the peace in his land.

A MAJOR MOVE

So the king simply kicked those cooks out of the kitchen. He restricted (divided up) the country and reduced the number of nomarchs big-time. Now there would be just three large districts, which were run by a council overseen by the king's vizier. This move created new jobs, established central departments dedicated to agriculture, the military, and the treasury—and strengthened Egypt across the board. Senwosret III's system was so successful that it stayed in place for hundreds of years—and kept Egypt afloat even under the rule of some less-than-fantastic pharaohs.

WARRIOR KING

Pharaohs often doubled as war heroes, and Senwosret III was no exception. He was swift and smart, and absolutely crushed his competition on the battlefield. It certainly helped that Egypt was quite the powerhouse in those days, but Senwosret III's leadership made the country that much more dominant.

Intent on extending Egypt's power beyond its borders, Senwosret III focused on Nubia, a neighboring land rich in gold. First, he had a canal built on the Nile for easier access to Nubia. Then, he invaded the country a whopping *five* times. Each battle broke Nubia down a bit more, until he was able to completely conquer it. This victory expanded Egypt's borders farther south than ever before.

SENWOSRET III BUILT THE **LARGEST** KNOWN **UNDERGROUND TOMB,** INCLUDING A GREAT HALL THAT WAS AS **LONG** AS A **BOWLING LANE.**

AFTER SENWOSRET III CONQUERED NUBIA, THIS LAND WAS ALL HIS.

ART SHOWING SOLDIERS IN ANCIENT EGYPT SPEAKING WITH A MERCHANT OUTSIDE A FORT

CELEB STATUS

Surprisingly, the Nubians weren't mad about this new king taking over their land. Quite the opposite! They actually worshipped him as a god and dedicated a cult just to him—a very rare honor for a still living pharaoh. And Senwosret III didn't have fans following him just in Nubia—his own people were just as obsessed and built temples and giant statues in his honor. Yep, you could say he was definitely a big deal.

FIERCE FORTRESSES

To keep his newly expanded land as safe as possible, Senwosret III built a chain of mighty fortresses in Nubia. And he wasn't messing around! This king had some eight fortresses built in one 40-mile (64-km) span, with potentially many others still undiscovered. These fortresses served as a barrier of protection from any potential invasions. To really set his thoughts in, uh, stone, Senwosret III placed a pair of stelae—or monumental slabs—on the border, etched with hieroglyphs proclaiming Egypt's dominance over Nubia and asking successors to keep the border safe.

KEEPING IT REAL

In nearly every work of ancient art depicting Senwosret III, he is shown to be rather worried—and wrinkled. In fact, he's one of the only pharaohs to appear anything but confident and youthful in art. Why so sad? Some say Senwosret's sourpuss expression isn't meant to be a reflection of a weak or glum king, but perhaps shows a hardworking, shrewd leader who had great concern for his people. Other experts believe that Senwosret III's sculptors were simply showcasing that this great king was older—and wiser, too.

This is just how I smile

Hatshepsut
The First Known FEMALE PHARAOH

PRINCESS POWER

Hatshepsut was born to rule. The daughter of one king and the wife of another, this princess had all the tools needed to be a powerful Egyptian leader. The only issue? She was a woman! But Hatshepsut didn't let that stop her from grabbing the crown. When her husband, Thutmose II, died suddenly, she declared herself pharaoh since his heir—her stepson—was too young to rule. This move placed her among the first great women we know about from ancient history.

FLEXING HER MUSCLE

Hatshepsut wasn't only a confident queen, but a perceptive one, too. And because she was breaking new ground as a female ruler, she likely had an inkling that she'd be taken more seriously if she looked like the pharaohs before her. So she dressed in menswear, wore a false beard, and was always painted to look more masculine—fake muscles and all. But experts believe that Hatshepsut probably didn't want people to think she was a man. Rather, she was just following the styles set by other pharaohs.

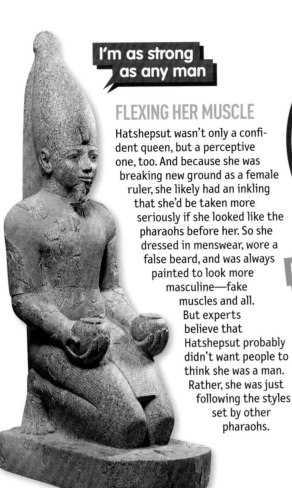

MUMMY MYSTERY: CASE OF THE MISSING TOOTH

In 1903, archaeologist Howard Carter discovered Hatshepsut's sarcophagus, or coffin, in a tomb within the Valley of the Kings. But there was just one problem: It was empty. It wasn't until 2007 when Hatshepsut's mummified remains were finally revealed.

And the discovery came about in the wackiest way. You see, for centuries, experts had been hanging on to the mummy of an anonymous woman in the hopes they could eventually figure out who she was. Meanwhile, a team of researchers came across a single molar tooth in a box with other items belonging to Hatshepsut. After noticing a gap in the mystery mummy's upper jaw, the experts thought they'd check to see if the tooth fit into the space. Turns out, it was a perfect fit—and the long search for the missing queen was finally over.

AWESOME EXPEDITIONS

As pharaoh, Hatshepsut wasn't content with just wearing the crown. She wanted to make history. And she started by overseeing major expeditions to far-off places like the Horn of Africa. You see, unlike the warrior pharaohs before her, Hatshepsut felt she could expand Egypt's power by building relationships with other countries through trade. So instead of waging war, she had fleets of boats built that were strong enough to sail the seas and sent thousands of men from her army off to explore new territories (she even went on some trips herself). The voyages may have been long—some took more than three years!—and challenging, but they reaped mega rewards for Egypt.

ABOUT FACE

Hello, Hatshepsut! A team of experts recently came across a 3,500-year-old stone fragment that had been sitting in storage for 40 years. This limestone carving, probably removed from a temple or a tomb, depicts part of a woman's face, which is believed to belong to the mysterious leader. Another reason the discovery is so remarkable? It was fittingly made on International Women's Day in 2018.

TRADING UP

Hands down, Hatshepsut's most famous expedition was to a place called Punt (pronounced *poont*). There, she offered up desirable Egyptian items like weapons, jewelry, and tools, and she returned home with boats loaded with all sorts of luxury items like gold, ivory, ebony, leopard skins, and even baboons, which she kept as pets. It's said she brought back five shiploads of luxury items, including dozens of living frankincense and myrrh trees, which she had planted throughout the kingdom. The remains of those trees still stand among the ruins of the ancient temple built to honor her.

A SECRET SPOT

While Hatshepsut shared stories of this sparkling land of riches (scientists later found detailed images and symbols detailing the expedition—from the ships on the water to the Punt people presenting their items—on the walls of her temple), she never once revealed its location. In fact, experts still aren't sure exactly where this place is, and some even believe it was actually made up! But after studying maps and artifacts left behind, researchers believe they've traced Punt back to an area close to modern-day Eritrea, Ethiopia, or Somalia. But others believe the real location may forever remain a secret Hatshepsut took with her to her tomb.

TOP TEMPLE

Meanwhile, back at home, Hatshepsut stayed just as busy overseeing the building of massive temples to honor the gods (and herself). Among her most stand-out structures? Hatshepsut's temple at Deir el-Bahri, which took 15 years to complete. The temple still stands and has three levels and features enormous statues of—who else?—Hatshepsut herself.

ERASING HISTORY

Hatshepsut's 20-some years as pharaoh were unforgettable. But her legacy was almost erased after she died around the age of 50. For starters, her stepson, likely jealous of Hatshepsut's success on what he believed was *his* throne, destroyed or damaged her monuments and anything bearing her name. He even went as far as building a big wall around some of her monuments to keep them hidden from plain sight. Later on, other pharaohs continued to remove her images from monuments in an attempt to erase any history of her reign. But Hatshepsut's contributions couldn't be silenced forever. In 1822, scholars decoded her name on the walls of her temple in Deir el-Bahri—and revealed just how powerful a force she really had been.

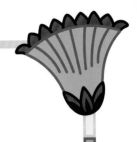

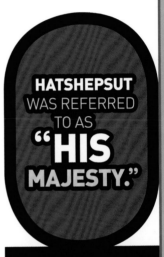

HATSHEPSUT WAS REFERRED TO AS **"HIS MAJESTY."**

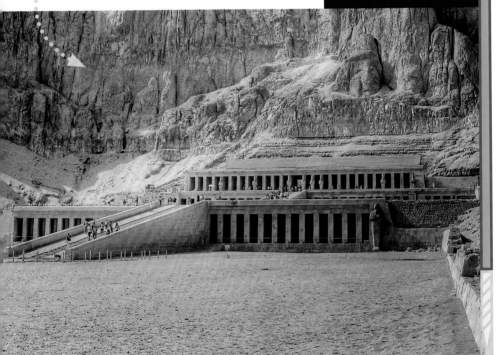

6 More Fierce Females
Other Women Who ROCKED IN ANCIENT EGYPT!

No doubt, ancient Egyptian women were way ahead of their time. Not only did some women rule the country as pharaohs, but they also had other higher-ranking positions in society. Even if they weren't nobility, women could own property, divorce and remarry, serve on juries, and testify in court—all opportunities not seen in other cultures until centuries later.

Throughout history, some women really stood out for being savvy and smart, and for simply knowing their stuff. Here are six females who totally rocked.

PESESHET

ALSO KNOWN AS:
The world's earliest known female physician

WHY SHE'S FIERCE:
A prominent doctor, Peseshet oversaw all other physicians of her time. She's also said to have created her own medications, performed surgeries, and possibly treated types of cancer.

NEBET

ALSO KNOWN AS: One of ancient Egypt's few female viziers

WHY SHE'S FIERCE: After learning to read and write as a kid, Nebet rose to the ranking of vizier. Considered the most powerful person after the king, she made important decisions on his behalf.

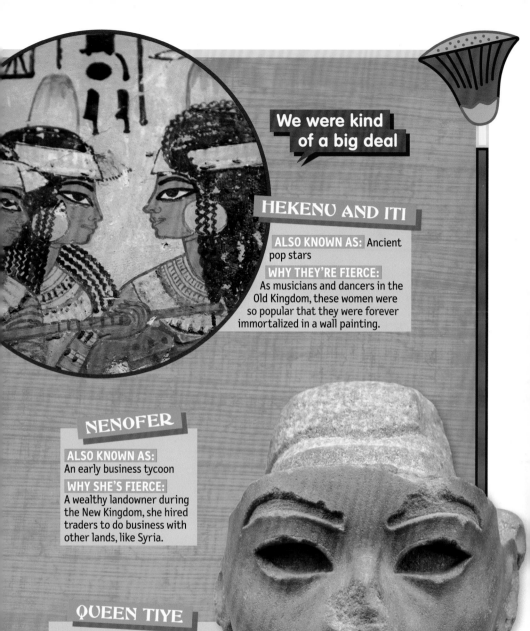

We were kind of a big deal

HEKENU AND ITI

ALSO KNOWN AS: Ancient pop stars

WHY THEY'RE FIERCE: As musicians and dancers in the Old Kingdom, these women were so popular that they were forever immortalized in a wall painting.

NENOFER

ALSO KNOWN AS: An early business tycoon

WHY SHE'S FIERCE: A wealthy landowner during the New Kingdom, she hired traders to do business with other lands, like Syria.

QUEEN TIYE

ALSO KNOWN AS: The Elder Lady

WHY SHE'S FIERCE: With an education worthy of a king, Tiye, the wife of pharaoh Amenhotep III, played an active role in the politics of Egypt and foreign relations. She is the first known Egyptian queen whose name appears in official acts.

Akhenaten & Nefertiti

The Couple Who CHANGED ANCIENT EGYPT'S RELIGION

WHEN: 1353–1336 B.C.
WHY THEY'RE WEIRD:
Every day, this couple rode their chariots from one end of their city to the other, echoing the sun's journey across the sky.

I'm a rebel
WITH a cause

NEW RELIGION

Talk about tunnel vision! Akhenaten had such a laser-like focus on his favorite god, Aten, that he changed his name from Amenhotep IV to honor him. He also spent nearly all of his time on the throne trying to please this sun god (read more about Egyptian mythology on page 102). Before he became pharaoh, all of Egypt worshipped many gods, much like the ancient Greeks did. But Akhenaten had other plans. He wanted his people to worship *only* Aten. This meant completely changing the country's religion.

A POWERFUL PARTNER

Akhenaten's religious rules may have been radical, but he was able to enforce them with the help of his wife, Queen Nefertiti. As the second most powerful person in ancient Egypt at the time, Nefertiti held most of the civilization in the palm of her hand. There may have been a bit of fear mixed in with that fandom, too—defying the pharaoh or his queen could lead to death.

AKHENATEN IS SOMETIMES CALLED " THE **ENEMY**" **IN EGYPTIAN RECORDS.**

Akhetaten didn't have the staying power of, say, Thebes, but the ruins of this ancient city remain. And thanks to a team dedicated to preserving the site, it's still around to check out today. Now it's known as the archaeological site Amarna, situated some 225 miles (362 km) south of Cairo. The area was first discovered back in the late 19th century, and, since then, archaeologists have worked to preserve as much as they can of this ancient area, including the family tombs of Akhenaten. They've also reconstructed some parts that had been damaged by weather—or by later pharaohs' attempts to destroy the lingering effects of Akhenaten's radical rule.

CAPITAL GAINS

To set their plan in motion, Akhenaten and Nefertiti shuttered temples dedicated to the other gods and cursed their names. They even built a new capital city called Akhetaten, in honor of the sun god. This was no easy feat. The site Akhenaten chose for this sacred spot—about 230 miles (370 km) from the former capital of Thebes—was an uninhabited, sandy swath of land on the Nile's east bank surrounded by desert cliffs. In just about five years, some 20,000 workers created a capital out of virtually nothing.

To save time, they made most of the buildings out of mud brick instead of stone. They built at least four palaces, hundreds of homes, and massive tombs cut out of rock. Temples were left open to the sky, so that the sun god's rays could reach them in the afterlife. Akhenaten and Nefertiti would have festivals inside the grandest temple, complete with music and other entertainment. Fancy!

THE SAD TRUTH

While the city is shown to be heaven-like and full of sunshine in ancient art, reality may have been quite the opposite. Studies on skeletons in Akhetaten's cemetery for commoners show bodies—some of them children—that had been battered by backbreaking work. Many of those buried had broken bones and other signs of hard labor. They were also malnourished, and experts think this means that these people were literally worked to the bone.

A QUEEN TAKEOVER

No pharaoh lived forever, and Akhenaten passed away not much longer after his new capital was built. Because Nefertiti was already officiating religious services and meeting with foreign VIPs while her husband ruled, it's thought she simply continued these duties on her own until she died some six years later. Experts say she also spent some of that time grooming a new pharaoh, none other than the future king Tutankhamun.

ALL FOR NOTHING?

Once both Akhenaten and Nefertiti passed away, it didn't take long for their unpopular religious beliefs to be struck down. The religious changes were reversed, and the capital city moved back to Thebes. Eventually, Akhetaten was abandoned. Forever more, Akhenaten's rule was marred by his radical move of going against the traditional gods.

NEFERTITI UNMASKED!

In art, Nefertiti is portrayed as tall and slender, with angular cheekbones. But after taking a deeper look at the legendary leader's bust, scientists say they've found that the famous sculpture may be masking the truth about her looks. High-tech scans of the bust's inner facial cast—made from an impression of Nefertiti's actual face—reveal she had wrinkles around her mouth and eyes and even a small bump on her nose. Just goes to show, even the royals aren't perfect!

DIG IT!
This 3,400-year-old bust of Nefertiti is considered to be the best known work of art from ancient Egypt.

King Tutankhamun
The Famous BOY KING

WHEN: 1332–1322 B.C.
WHY HE'S WEIRD:
He ruled Egypt for just
10 years but is still
among the most
famous pharaohs.

TUT TALES

For as famous as King Tut is today, there's practically no written record of him in ancient texts. So what do we know about this mysterious king and how do we know it? Well, genetic testing has verified that King Tut was the grandson of the great pharaoh Amenhotep III, and probably the son of Akhenaten. And his tomb—discovered remarkably intact—has revealed even more about this boy king, who took the throne around the age of nine after the death of his dad.

ARTISTIC REPRESENTATION OF THE RUINS OF THE GREAT TEMPLE AT KARNAK

Around 1914, archaeologist and Egyptologist Howard Carter was hired by a wealthy British royal, Lord Carnarvon, to head to Egypt and find artifacts to fill museums—and his castle. Carter worked for several years with no luck, since so many tombs had been raided by robbers long before he came upon them. Disappointed, Carnarvon prepared to call off the excavation. But Carter had a hunch he was close to coming upon something amazing, and he convinced his boss to give him one more year to dig. Just days later, Carter found a stone staircase in a yet-to-be-explored area in the Valley of the Kings. In February 1922, Carter pried open the door and revealed King Tut's tomb and his treasures. Making headlines around the world, the discovery was called "the most extraordinary day in the whole history of Egyptian excavation."

CREATING CHANGE

Even though he was believed to be the son of Akhenaten (and raised by Nefertiti, although experts believe she wasn't his biological mom), it seems he, or more likely his advisers, didn't share his parents' obsession with monotheism, or worshipping a single god. For starters, he was given the name Tutankhaten (meaning "the living image of Aten") at birth, only to change it to Tutankhamun (honoring Amun, the king of the gods). And whether he or his advisers were responsible, a big change did occur: When he came to the throne, the old gods who had been banished by his parents were brought back, and the Egyptians abandoned the city of Akhetaten for good, returning the capital to Thebes. He restored the holy sites that his father had attempted to destroy and built famous sites, like Karnak Temple. As a result, Tut became a symbol of change throughout Egypt.

HOWARD CARTER DISCOVERED KING TUT'S TOMB IN THE VALLEY OF THE KINGS IN 1922.

Using modern technology, including CT scans, DNA testing, x-rays, and computer-imaging technology, experts have examined Tut's mummy several times in an attempt to reach a conclusion about just how he died so young. The most plausible theory? That he contracted malaria, a deadly disease, which could've made him so weak that he ultimately fell and hurt himself so badly that he died a short time later. But much like the mystery that surrounds this famous pharaoh's life, we may never know how he died.

IT TOOK **10 YEARS** TO **REMOVE** AND **CATALOG** ALL **5,398 ITEMS** IN KING TUT'S **TOMB.**

PAMPERED PRINCE

Born a prince, Tut received the royal treatment from day one, spending his time toddling around his lavish palace, swimming in pools the size of lakes, playing his beloved board games, listening to live music, and eating feasts of meats, vegetables, and sweets. Servants tended to Tut all day, bathing him, dressing him, and even fanning him with ostrich plumes to beat the dry desert heat. Even though Tut likely attended a special school just for royals, he had a lot of help in the classroom. After all, he had scribes to write down his every thought. Must've been nice!

ON THE HUNT

One of Tut's favorite hobbies? Ostrich hunting! Back in the day, ostriches were prized for their feathers and eggs, and experts think he spent a lot of his time chasing the giant birds in his chariot. A fan made from ostrich feathers was found in his burial chamber, and on its handle is written a story about a time when the king caught the bird in a desert near the town of Heliopolis.

BOY SOLDIER?

Tut was trained in the military, and a new study shows that he may have spent time on the battlefield. After analyzing a coat of armor made of leather found in his tomb, experts noticed that the edging of it was worn down—a sign it may have gotten some use in war. There was also a wooden box painted with a scene of Tut leading a charge against the Nubians and Syrians over territories and control of trade routes. Whether or not Tut was a warrior king, we may never know. But these items—and his love of hunting—show that he was likely a fairly active pharaoh before falling sick as a teenager.

A SUDDEN ENDING

As Tut grew older, he may have had the chance to take on more control of his country, but studies of his mummy show that he was pretty sick toward the end of his life. Weakened by an infection or malaria, experts say Tut was unable to walk without a cane when he died at the age of 19. His illness came on rather suddenly, and experts think he was buried in a tomb meant for someone else—maybe Queen Nefertiti—since no one was expecting such a young pharaoh to die.

10 Kooky Items

1 A lock of his grand-mother's hair

2 Hundreds of pairs of royal underpants

3 Sandals with his enemies painted on the soles (so he could stomp on the competition!)

4 A dismantled golden chariot

5 Jars containing Tut's organs, removed before the mummification process

6 Throwing sticks, similar to boomerangs (so he could hunt birds in the afterlife)

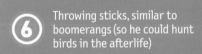

7 Perfume

8 A dagger made out of meteorite iron

9 Licorice

10 Watermelon seeds

CURSES!

When Howard Carter opened the door to King Tut's tomb, he unleashed a worldwide obsession for ancient Egypt—and, some believe, a curse. Not only were people fascinated by this young king and the heaps of glittering treasures he was buried with, but they also dreamed up far-fetched ideas about this ancient civilization. Among those? That his mummy was cursed—and anyone who messed with it would be subject to a royal dose of bad luck, or worse ...

A DEADLY BITE. Just four months after the Tut discovery, George Herbert, Lord of Carnarvon, the wealthy man who backed Carter's expedition, died of blood poisoning from an infected mosquito bite. At the moment of his death, Cairo experienced a blackout. Newspaper headlines at the time screamed about the curse of the mummy, which was seeking retaliation on anyone who disturbed its tomb.

A HOUSE FIRE. An American Egyptologist named Aaron Ember, who was present when the tomb was opened, perished in a house fire after he went in to save a manuscript about the Egyptian *Book of the Dead*.

A SUDDEN ILLNESS. Wealthy railroad executive George Jay Gould fell sick and died soon after visiting the tomb in 1923.

FACT CHECK! Just a coincidence? Truth is, Lord Carnarvon was said to be in bad health at the time of the discovery, and Carter himself lived for another 20 years. And the other incidents may have been pure coincidences. More of the 26 people who were there for the tomb's opening died of mysterious causes, but only six of them passed within a decade. While some people still believe in the mummy's curse—most likely, it's just a myth.

FACT OR FICTION? You Decide! A Closer Look at the CURSE OF KING TUT'S TOMB

HOWARD CARTER AND HIS EGYPTIAN ASSISTANT EXAMINE THE SARCOPHAGUS OF KING TUT IN 1925.

Ramses II

THE MOST POWERFUL PHARAOH
of the Egyptian Empire

WHEN: 1279–1213 B.C.

WHY HE'S WEIRD:
He lived to see his 96th birthday—and outlived 12 of his crown princes.

THE RULER OF RULERS

There's a reason they called Ramses II "The Great." He spent more than 65 years on the throne—one of the longest reigns in Egyptian history! The son of pharaoh Seti I, Ramses would tag along with his dad to battles. This set him up to become a talented and smart military leader. By the time he took the throne from his father, he was totally ready to rule.

ARRR, PIRATES!

In just his second year as pharaoh, Ramses II went after a gang of pirates who were attacking Egypt's ships at sea. And he pulled off the defeat in a pretty sneaky way: First, he stationed ships and troops along the coast as decoys. When the pirates went after the ships, Ramses II and his soldiers swooped in with a surprise attack. They eventually captured all of the pirates and, well, sank their enemies at sea for good.

A BITTER BATTLE

Ramses II gained major momentum as a ruler by battling with the best of them—meaning Egypt's fiercest competitors. Among its rivals were the Hittites—a neighboring empire that is modern-day Turkey—who wanted control of trade routes and to take over the city of Kadesh. In what's considered the earliest recorded battle, Ramses gathered some 20,000 troops to face off against the Hittite army, which was more than twice the size of the Egyptian forces. At one point, Ramses II barely escaped an ambush by the Hittite army before leading his troops in a counterattack and ultimately forcing the enemy out of Egypt.

RAMSES II HAD **RED HAIR.**

MODERN ART DEPICTING THE BATTLE OF KADESH

How do you move a giant 3,200-year-old statue? Very carefully! When a granite sculpture of Ramses II was relocated from a storage unit to its new home in the Grand Egyptian Museum in Giza, Egypt, it was truly a royal affair. First, a team of engineers built a custom-made metal cage around the three-story-high statue (which weighs more than 12 elephants). Then, they lifted it onto two trailer beds attached to a truck. Crowds cheered as the truck moved at a turtle's pace some 1,300 feet (396 m) down the street en route to the museum. This wasn't the first time the statue had been moved: When it was transferred some 25 miles (40 km) from the ruins to Cairo, it's said that the Giza Zoo's lions roared when the statue passed by.

HISTORY, OR *HIS STORY?*

As for who actually won the Battle of Kadesh, well, that depends on who you ask. Both sides claimed victory—and Ramses had his people report back to Egypt that they, in fact, had won the four-day battle. Whether tall tale or truth, one thing is for sure: Ramses was eventually able to secure peace with the Hittites. The two sides signed a peace treaty agreeing to finally stop the skirmishes between them.

PEACE OUT

This wasn't just any peace treaty, though. It was the world's first! And it was literally written in stone—and silver. They made two copies of the treaty, one in hieroglyphs etched into a silver plaque and the other in Akkadian, the language of the Hittites, written on a stone tablet. The two sides agreed to never attack each other again—a promise kept for the rest of Ramses II's reign and until the fall of the Hittite empire.

ONE OF THE WORLD'S FIRST PEACE TREATIES, ETCHED IN CLAY

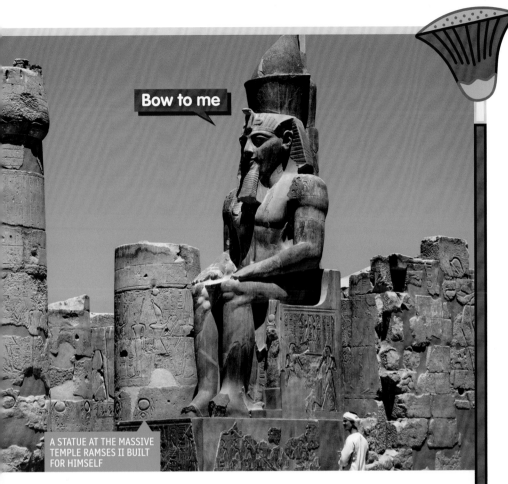

Bow to me

A STATUE AT THE MASSIVE TEMPLE RAMSES II BUILT FOR HIMSELF

NAME GAME

Ramses wanted people to remember him for a long, long time. So this sneaky leader added his name to messages in monuments dedicated to former pharaohs and also had his people build many monuments and temples dedicated to him—more than any other Egyptian leader. Among these? The massive Ramesseum temple complex in Thebes and the Great Temple at Abu Simbel. Four giant statues of Ramses II guard the front of Abu Simbel, each standing as tall as a six-story building!

EGYPTIAN IDOL

Build a bunch of big temples and statues in your name and people will talk about you for centuries, right? Well, that plan worked for Ramses II! Some of those statues still stand today. And Ramses II was so revered that nine future pharaohs called themselves Ramses in the hopes of snagging some of his success, though none of them actually, well, lived up to the name.

A NEW RULE

The Egyptians flourished on their own as a powerful country for thousands of years. But not even the greatest kingdoms can stay at the top forever. Constant invasions and battles with other lands, infighting among Egypt's central government, and the death of Ramses II all weakened the Egyptian Empire and left it exposed to outsiders. Eventually, the country came under the control of foreign leaders, including Persia, which loosely ruled it for more than 100 years.

ALONG CAME ALEXANDER. Alexander the Great, a king from ancient Greece (then known as Macedonia), stepped in, seeking to expand his empire. In 332 B.C., he defeated the Persians to take over Egypt as the new leader of the land. He went to work quickly, establishing a new capital called, well, Alexandria. Sitting at the mouth of the Nile River, Alexandria soon became one of the most powerful cities in the world—and an education epicenter, with one of the most famous libraries ever built (read more about it on page 134).

A SHORT STAY. Alexander was greatly respected by the Egyptians, who saw him as a demigod. He was dazzled by some of their customs and even adopted certain traditions, like sacrificing to their gods. But he wasn't much for sticking in one place for too long, and just a year after conquering Egypt, he left to continue his conquest of the Persian Empire. Later, one of his generals, named Ptolemy, claimed Egypt as his kingdom and set up his own dynasty, which meant the Greeks continued to rule until the Romans conquered the country 300 years later.

A LASTING LEGACY. By the time of his death, Alexander the Great had amassed the largest empire in the entire ancient world, spanning some 3,000 miles (4,828 km). It's said that when he died, his body was embalmed in honey and taken to Alexandria to be buried. Today, the city of Alexandria still stands, serving as a lasting legacy for this powerful leader.

A MOSQUE IN MODERN-DAY ALEXANDRIA

ANCIENT EGYPT Loses Its Independence and Gets a NEW CAPITAL

A DEPICTION OF THE CAPITAL CITY DURING ITS HEYDAY

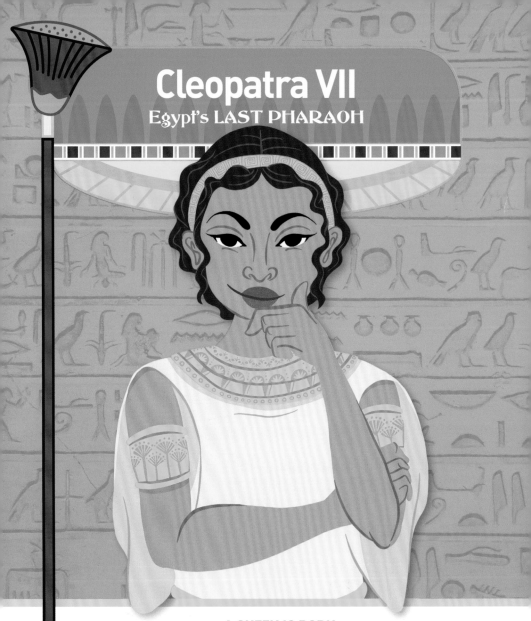

Cleopatra VII
Egypt's LAST PHARAOH

A QUEEN IS BORN

After Alexander the Great conquered Egypt, the country was ruled by foreign monarchs, who hailed mostly from Macedonia. One of these was Cleopatra VII, a teen queen who followed her father, Ptolemy XII, to the throne. As a kid, Cleopatra was groomed for royal glory. She attended school in Alexandria, Egypt, and learned to speak as many as seven languages, becoming the first in her family to learn Egyptian (they'd been speaking Greek for more than 250 years!). Her smarts set her up nicely for her royal role, but her trip to the top wasn't without plenty of drama.

74

OH, BROTHER!

Standing in Cleopatra's way? None other than her very own brother. When their father died, he left the throne to both his daughter and his son, Ptolemy XIII, who was just around 10 years old at the time. As the older sister, Cleopatra figured she had the pharaoh role, but Ptolemy's advisers weren't so giddy about having a female leader. So they pushed Ptolemy onto the throne and forced Cleopatra out of Egypt to nearby Syria.

FIGHTING BACK

But Cleopatra wasn't about to give that throne up so easily. After being booted from Egypt by her brother, Cleopatra gathered a crew of mercenaries—or hired soldiers—to join her army. Mostly made up of Greeks, Romans, and Persians, she paid the soldiers in gold. She also teamed up with famous Roman general and dictator Julius Caesar, a powerful leader whom she figured could help her take her brother down.

CLEOPATRA WAS ACTUALLY **GREEK, NOT EGYPTIAN.**

Bring it on

CLEOPATRA LEADING HER CREW INTO BATTLE

ROLL WITH IT

You see, at the time, the Romans had taken control of Egypt, even though they still let the Greeks lead the country. And as a top-notch Roman general, Caesar had made his way to Egypt, partly to decide whether Cleopatra should have solo rule over the country. By then, Cleopatra had returned to Egypt with her troops in tow and was ready to do whatever it took to take the throne. She knew she needed Caesar on her side. So, according to the ancient writer Plutarch, Cleopatra wooed Caesar by sneaking into his apartment hidden inside a rolled-up carpet. Once she popped out of the rug and Caesar locked eyes on her, he was instantly smitten and agreed to help Cleopatra lead a charge against her brother.

IT'S LOVE! CLEOPATRA AND CAESAR ONLY HAD EYES FOR EACH OTHER.

THIS MEANS WAR!

Ptolemy flipped when he found out about his sister's sneaky act. He quickly rounded up his troops and readied himself for battle, which took place on the shores of the Nile River. The victory didn't come easily for Caesar, even if he was known as the world's greatest general. Ptolemy's troops put up a tough fight day after day, battling under the blazing sun. Finally, on March 27, 47 B.C., Caesar made one final push to force the Egyptians toward the Nile, where he rendered his rivals helpless. In an attempt to flee the fighting, Ptolemy is said to have drowned in the Nile when his ship capsized. That sealed a win for Caesar's side—and Cleopatra. That crown? *All* hers.

DIG IT!
Cleopatra's daughter Cleopatra Selene went on to rule the ancient region of Mauretania, in northwest Africa.

A LOYAL ROYAL

So what made Cleopatra such a stand-out queen? Even though she was Greek, she embraced Egyptian traditions and worshipped their gods—and this loyalty made her extremely popular among her people. Her face was even on their coins! As a result, the country prospered and life was pretty good for most of Cleopatra's reign.

Et tu, guys?

DEATH OF CAESAR · · · ·

As beloved as Cleopatra was in Egypt, the Romans weren't quite so crazy about her— especially when it came to her relationship with their leader. And this unsavory outlook on her may have helped lead to Caesar's demise. In 44 B.C., just as Caesar was planning to marry Cleopatra and name their son, Caesarion, his heir, he was murdered. This just so happened to occur at a time when Cleopatra was visiting Rome. Some call it a coincidence, while others think his death was directly linked to Cleopatra.

Cleopatra may have died long ago, but her legend is still making waves. Really! In the 1990s, underwater archaeologist Franck Goddio and his team found her former home at the bottom of the Mediterranean Sea. The submerged royal quarters wound up in the sea off the shores of Alexandria, Egypt, after a series of tsunamis and earthquakes. Among the 20,000 items found in these sunken royal quarters? Pieces of pottery, gold coins, and a 2.5-foot (.76-m)-tall stone head believed to have once belonged to a statue of Cleopatra's son, Caesarion. While a lot of the artifacts have been brought to the surface to be examined and put on display, some of the stuff still remains in this watery grave.

A LIVING GODDESS

Cleopatra was one confident queen! She believed she was the reincarnation of the Egyptian god Isis and went to great lengths to prove it. Like the time she dressed up like a beautiful goddess to meet Roman general and statesman Mark Antony, who was Caesar's right-hand man and had great influence on the Roman Empire. After Caesar died, she wanted to woo Antony in order to keep her alliance with the Romans—and her tight hold on Egypt.

As the story goes, Cleopatra arrived in Tarsus, where Antony lived, floating on a golden barge with purple sails and rowed by silver oars. There, she sat on a golden canopy while attendants dressed as cupids fanned her and the strains of music from flutes and harps wafted over the water. The ruse worked—Antony fell in love with her, and the two of them married.

Egypt's mine

ROMAN RIVALS

With Antony by her side, Cleopatra's empire grew. He helped her extinguish her enemies and gave her land. But it was also a very tumultuous time—and love could not conquer all.

Enter Octavian, the ruthless Roman leader—and legal heir of Julius Caesar—who wanted to take over Egypt. Cleopatra boldly accepted the challenge. At the famous naval battle at Actium off the western coast of Greece in 31 B.C., Cleopatra led a fleet of Egyptian warships to clash against Octavian. Mark Antony joined her, but the two could not overtake Octavian. After heavy fighting—and the loss of some 5,000 sailors— Cleopatra and Antony called it quits and retreated to Egypt. Soon after, Antony died. A devastated and heartbroken Cleopatra claimed that she'd rather die than hand over her kingdom to the Romans.

END OF AN EMPIRE

You can't say Cleopatra wasn't a woman of her word. After being defeated by the Roman Empire, she carefully planned out her death, which would mark the end of the Egyptians' empire for good. According to legend, the queen smuggled a snake known as an asp in a small basket into her already-built tomb and then enticed it to bite her arm. But some experts say this is just a tall tale. While no one knows for sure how Cleopatra died, scientists say she may have downed a toxic cocktail or pricked herself with a needle dipped in poison. Ouch!

BIG SPENDERS

Mark Antony and Cleopatra were definitely party people. Surviving accounts tell of lavish dinners, late-night parties, and no concern for cost whatsoever. One story says Cleopatra once dissolved one of her pearl earrings in vinegar and drank it with her meal—just to prove to her husband that she could host the world's most expensive dinner party. With the earring being worth what would be millions in today's dollars, that must've been one pricey party.

The Pyramids
The FAMOUS EGYPTIAN TOMBS
That Are Totally ON POINT

THE GREAT PYRAMID AT GIZA IS THE TALLEST PYRAMID IN EGYPT.

DIG IT!
The Great Pyramid of Khufu stood as the world's tallest human-made structure for nearly 4,000 years.

What's one way to make sure you'll be remembered forever? Build the biggest, tallest tomb to yourself—and make sure it can stand the test of time. That's just what many of ancient Egypt's pharaohs did. Many of the hundreds of pyramids built in ancient times are still standing as lingering symbols of the pharaohs' legacies.

Plain and simple, pyramids were tombs for the pharaohs. Instead of being buried underground or in a smaller space, these kings created these triangular structures with a square base and four sides to protect their bodies and all of their treasures.

WHO BUILT THE PYRAMIDS?

For centuries, the assumption was that slaves or prisoners constructed the pyramids. But more recent studies show that many of the laborers were farmers who devoted their off-season (the four months when the Nile flooded) to constructing these giant tombs for their kings. They were paid in food and clothes, and the government provided meals, housing, and tools as they toiled away.

BEHIND THE BUILD

Building a pyramid was a team effort! First, workers had to dig up limestone from the desert. Then, stonemasons had to cut and shape millions of limestone blocks by hand. Groups of workers would haul these stones to the pyramid site using ropes, sleds, and ramps—a Herculean task considering each stone weighed more than two tons! All told, it took some 25,000 skilled laborers, including architects, engineers, builders, and craftsmen, to pull off a pyramid.

IMHOTEP'S ORIGINAL DESIGN

Not all pharaohs had pyramids. In fact, King Djoser, of the 3rd dynasty, had the first ever pyramid built some 4,500 years ago, and it still stands today. An architect named Imhotep is credited with the original design, which featured six rectangles stacked on top of each other, each getting smaller toward the top.

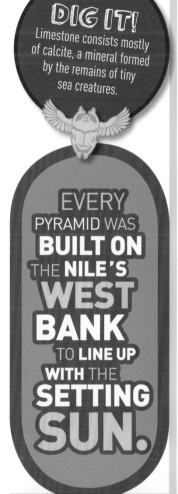

DIG IT! Limestone consists mostly of calcite, a mineral formed by the remains of tiny sea creatures.

EVERY PYRAMID WAS **BUILT ON** THE **NILE'S WEST BANK** TO **LINE UP** WITH THE **SETTING SUN.**

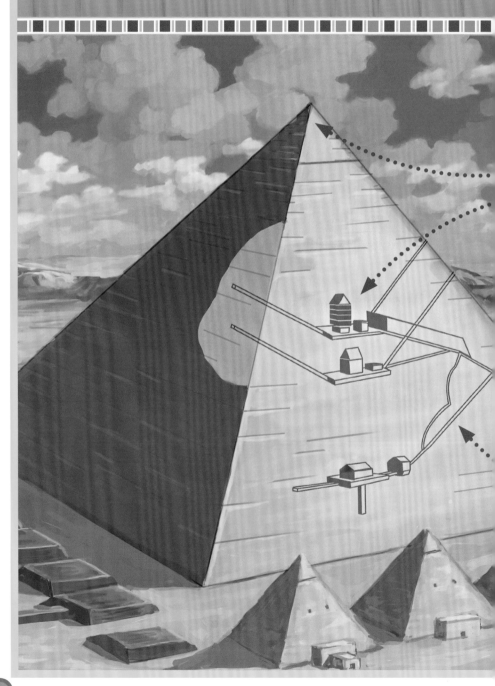

The Main Features of THESE FASCINATING STRUCTURES

ON POINT. The highest point of the pyramid served as a symbolic launch pad for the soul following the pharaoh's death. From here, the soul would take off and travel to the afterlife. The point was covered by a capstone, usually covered in a mixture of gold and silver.

THE SHAPE OF IT ALL. The Egyptians believed that the pharaoh ascended to heaven on the rays of the sun, so the shape of the pyramid was a symbol for the sun's rays. After his or her burial, the pharaoh would climb up the pyramid to get to the afterlife.

RESTING PLACE. The pharaoh would have a burial chamber inside the pyramid. This huge room held the coffin—or sarcophagus—as well as any valuables.

SMOOTH SURFACE. The outer layer was made from polished white limestone blocks, giving the pyramid a smooth exterior.

A LOT OF LIMESTONE. Most pyramids were built out of limestone, which was likely hauled in on barges up the Nile River. Workers then moved the heavy stones by pushing wooden rollers up ramps built on the side of the structure.

PLENTY OF PASSAGES. A maze of long passages and tunnels was built within the pyramid, all leading to the king's burial chamber.

KEEP OUT. Some pyramids had several false doors cut into them. Inside some of these doors? A giant trench meant to trick—and trap—unwanted guests, like robbers.

TINY TOMBS. Many pyramids were surrounded by smaller pyramids that served as tombs for members of the royal family. Other structures, like the famous Great Sphinx, were built nearby as symbols of the powerful rulers buried within the tomb.

Pyramids

① STEP PYRAMID OF DJOSER

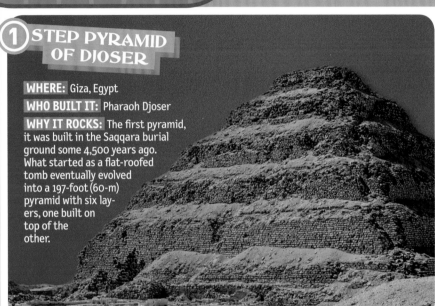

WHERE: Giza, Egypt

WHO BUILT IT: Pharaoh Djoser

WHY IT ROCKS: The first pyramid, it was built in the Saqqara burial ground some 4,500 years ago. What started as a flat-roofed tomb eventually evolved into a 197-foot (60-m) pyramid with six layers, one built on top of the other.

② BENT PYRAMID

WHERE: Dahshur, Egypt

WHO BUILT IT: Pharaoh Snefru

WHY IT ROCKS: As its name suggests, this pyramid's sides have a bent slope. The second-oldest pyramid in Egypt, it's unique shape is probably from a design flaw that occurred during construction, as the upper half of it was built at a lower angle than the bottom. It's the only pyramid in Egypt that still has a largely intact outer casing of polished limestone.

③ MEIDUM

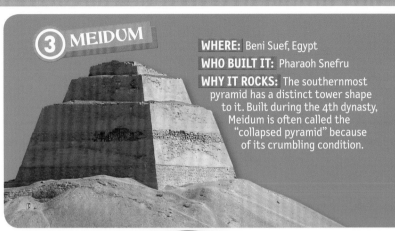

WHERE: Beni Suef, Egypt

WHO BUILT IT: Pharaoh Snefru

WHY IT ROCKS: The southernmost pyramid has a distinct tower shape to it. Built during the 4th dynasty, Meidum is often called the "collapsed pyramid" because of its crumbling condition.

④ PYRAMID OF KHUFU

WHERE: Giza, Egypt

WHO BUILT IT: Pharaoh Khufu

WHY IT ROCKS: Also known as the Great Pyramid, Khufu was more than 480 feet (146 m) tall when it was first built some 4,500 years ago. Over time, erosion and vandalism has lopped some 30 feet (9 m) off its height, but it still stands as the world's tallest pyramid.

DIG IT!
In the 19th century, European tourists paid local people to carry them up to the top of Khufu's pyramid.

⑤ PYRAMID OF KHAFRE

WHERE: Giza, Egypt

WHO BUILT IT: Pharaoh Khafre

WHY IT ROCKS: One of the main three pyramids in Giza, it's guarded by the famous Great Sphinx. Khafre's pyramid appears to be taller than the Great Pyramid at Giza, but only because it was built at a higher elevation.

THE TRUTH ABOUT TOMBS

Pyramids were a major focus for pharaohs for several hundred years. And then, over time, they stopped building these massive memorials in favor of tombs tucked away into cliffs surrounding the Valley of the Kings. So, what caused the shift?

A NEW STYLE.

Researchers say there are a few factors. First, the pyramid may have fallen out of fashion, with the Egyptians exploring different architectural styles. Or, the pyramids may also have cost too much to build. Another theory is that the Egyptians opted to hide their burial spots to stop looters from ransacking the tombs, which was a huge problem at the time.

BLAME THE WEATHER.

The main theory for why the pyramids phased out? The weather.

Typically, daytime temperatures in the Sahara rise to 104°F (40°C) and drop to 37°F (3°C) at night. Experts say this huge temperature swing caused a pyramid's smooth stones to expand and contract, also known as "thermal movement." As a result, the stones cracked and crumbled. While it's not unusual to see buildings wear down over time, researchers believe the pyramids showed signs of wear and tear soon after they were completed. And just imagine how frustrating it would be for the Egyptians to see the structures they spent so much time perfecting literally crumbling before their eyes! It might have been just enough to make them move on to tucked-away tombs.

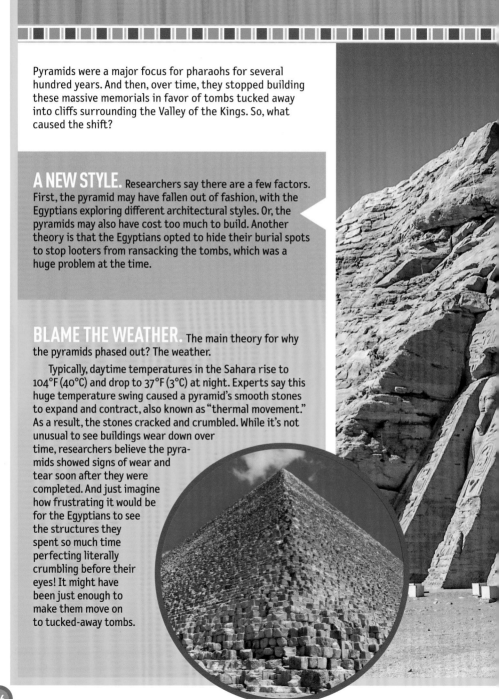

Why Egyptians STOPPED BUILDING
PYRAMIDS

THE NILE VALLEY IS HOME TO SOME OF THE GREATEST MONUMENTS OF THE ANCIENT WORLD.

Inside the Tombs
A Closer Look at Ancient Egypt's
TUCKED-AWAY BURIAL SPOTS

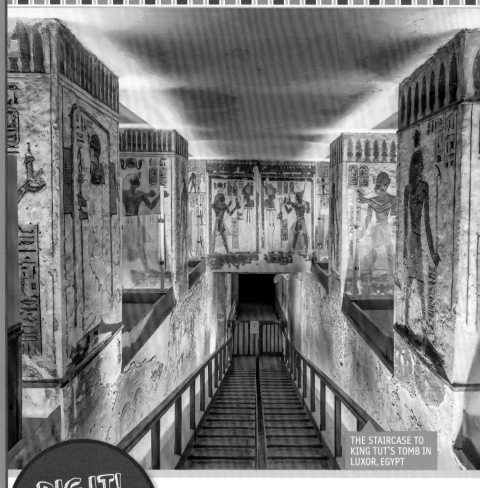

THE STAIRCASE TO KING TUT'S TOMB IN LUXOR, EGYPT

DIG IT!
In the Valley of the Kings, tomb entrances were disguised to prevent anyone from locating them.

TOMB BOOM

No important ancient Egyptian was ever buried six feet under. And after pyramids fell out of fashion, many pharaohs were laid to rest in hidden tombs in the rocky cliffs high above the Valley of the Kings. Located deep within the desert, this valley falls in the shadow of a mountain shaped like a pyramid. So, naturally, the Egyptians probably figured it would be the best place to bury their beloved leaders.

SET IN STONE

Unlike the pyramids, which were built in Lower Egypt, these tombs were constructed in the southern part of the country, in Thebes. Highly skilled stoneworkers would cut into the stony cliffs using handmade tools like bronze chisels and wooden hammers and create huge tombs for the pharaohs. Not only that, they'd decorate and furnish them, too, etching images into rock, including figures of the gods, animals, and scenes from nature. They'd create their own pigments using minerals and paint the tombs' walls in brilliant colors, and artisans would craft amenities like cosmetics and clothes to make sure a pharaoh was totally set up in comfort for the afterlife. All told, the process would take two years or longer to create one tomb. So the construction often began as soon as a new pharaoh took the throne to make sure it was ready to go when he or she was, well, ready to go.

BEWARE THE TOMB RAIDERS

These secret spots were meant to keep the pharaohs far away from the riffraff—and robbers. The Egyptians went to great lengths to keep them out of sight and secure, from building false entrances to secret chambers and passageways. Still, of the dozens of tombs discovered to date, nearly every single one has been ransacked by tomb raiders. Robbers stole everything from priceless jewels to strips of linen (which was more valuable than gold because it was easier to sell and harder to trace), leaving nothing but an empty, messy tomb behind. And if these criminals did get caught? They were beaten on the soles of their feet with a stick before being impaled slowly on a sharpened stake. *That'll* teach them.

ART IMITATES LIFE

How have scientists found out so much about the lives of the dead? The truth is in the tomb paintings! These highly detailed scenes offer a highlight reel of the deceased's life, showing him or her at their prime, before he or she got old and sick. Such scenes may show people dancing, playing musical instruments, and hunting—the types of activities that the dead person would likely want to do in the afterlife, too.

OVER THE YEARS, SOME TOMBS WERE RECYCLED AND REUSED FOR SEVERAL DIFFERENT PEOPLE.

Steal me, if you dare

Priest Power

Mummy Makers and SERVANTS OF THE GODS

DIG IT!

Every priest wore a mask of a jackal—or wild dog—while making a mummy.

SUPREME GO-BETWEEN

In ancient Egypt, the pharaoh was the top dog. But not far behind were high-ranking priests, who were basically the gatekeepers between the living and their beloved gods. They performed duties for the pharaoh, were in charge of mummification, oversaw funerals, and tended to temples dedicated to the gods. Yep, you could say that priests were pretty powerful.

A FAMILY AFFAIR

Not just anyone could propel themselves to the priesthood. The role of chief priest was often passed down from generation to generation within one family, in a similar manner to how pharaohs were selected. When a new priest was chosen, the king would send his messenger to inform the whole land. It was big news!

ALL ABOUT THE GODS

There's a reason that priests were called servants of the gods. They each had a laser-like focus on a particular god and spent a large part of their days making sure the god was satisfied. This included washing and dressing the sacred statue of the god stashed inside its temple every morning, offering it food and drink, burning incense in the god's honor, and keeping intruders away. Sure, feeding and bathing a statue may sound bizarre. But back then, these acts were an honor given only to the best of the best.

PRIESTESS WITH THE MOSTESS

Women could be priests, too! Although not very common, female priests—or priestesses—did pop up here and there. One such leader was Hetpet, who served as a priestess to Hathor, the goddess of love. Archaeologists recently discovered Hetpet's 4,000-year-old tomb, which was exquisitely decorated with paintings, including some scenes of her hunting and fishing. The tomb's size and lavish details underscore just how much priests—and priestesses— were respected and revered.

MUMMY MAKERS

Priests weren't just well versed in religion. They were highly educated and super smart, too. In fact, no Egyptian could become a priest without learning to read and write as a kid—and many continued their education to become judges, lawyers, and doctors, on top of being a priest! Because many priests had a good understanding of the human body, it made sense that they took charge of mummifying, too. They did everything from treating wounds to removing organs—all to get the body perfectly prepped for the afterlife.

ONE PRIEST, CALLED THE **"RIPPER UP,"** WAS IN CHARGE OF MAKING THE **FIRST CUT** INTO THE DEAD BODY.

An Epic Journey
The Ancient Egyptian's JOURNEY TO THE AFTERLIFE

AN IMAGE FROM THE *BOOK OF THE DEAD*

UNLIKE AVERAGE PEOPLE, **PHARAOHS** WERE SAID TO **FLY RIGHT** UP TO **HEAVEN** AND SAIL ACROSS THE SKY **FOREVER.**

PACKED AND READY TO GO

Pack that clean underwear! And don't forget your snacks! Preparation was everything when planning for life after death in ancient Egypt. Why? Because ancient Egyptians believed that a person could continue to live even after their last breath on Earth. So, of course, the person needed all sorts of essentials—from food to, yep, clean undies—to take along on the journey.

GETTING TO THE LAND OF THE DEAD

The afterlife was set in a blissful place where you'd find eternal happiness. But the journey to get there wasn't all that easy—and it didn't end well for everyone. To be totally prepared for the path to paradise, the ancient Egyptians studied the *Book of the Dead*, which laid out the rules for achieving afterlife success for the dead, plus tips for the living on prepping the body in the precise way that would please the gods.

Path to Paradise

① GET MUMMIFIED

The dead body is mummified by a team of priests who remove every organ except the heart. The heart, the Egyptians believed, was the source of emotion and intelligence—and a person's soul—so it was left with the body so the spirit could reunite with it in the afterlife.

Soul long

② TRAVEL TO THE UNDERWORLD

The spirit next passes through the underworld, a realm of fiery lakes, vast caverns, and magical gates guarded by snakes, crocodiles, and vicious monsters. Before dying, a properly prepared person would have studied up on a series of magical spells—outlined in the *Book of the Dead*—that could be used to defeat these demons.

③ SPEAK YOUR TRUTH

Once past the scary stuff, the dead meets up with the goddess of truth and justice. Here, the dead must prove that he or she has done nothing bad while alive. A jury of 42 lesser gods decides whether the dead is, in fact, good enough to ascend to the afterlife.

④ WEIGH YOUR HEART

Next, the dead's heart is weighed on a scale. A heart lighter than a feather (known as the Feather of Truth) passes the test and the dead moves on. But a heart heavier than a feather suggests that the dead's soul is weighed down by bad deeds and lies. In that case, the heart is devoured by Ammut, a monstrous mesh of a crocodile, hippo, and leopard. Game over.

⑤ ONE FINAL LOOK OVER

If the dead's heart is proved to be pure, the sun god swoops in and carries the person to Osiris, the god who guards the underworld. Osiris gives the final stamp of approval to enter the afterlife—where the dead is met by all of his or her loved ones who have passed before, from pets to family members, and the dead goes on to live in a heaven of endless goodies and eternal peace.

BY THE BOOK

It sounds like a prop out of a movie, but the ancient Egyptians used the *Book of the Dead* like a map to get into the afterlife. Not only did it outline all the ways to safely lead the soul past the underworld, but it contained some 200 spells to do just that. Though called books, these guides were actually individual chapters written on papyrus sheets or on the walls of tombs. Some versions of the *Book of the Dead* were over 100 feet (30 m) long!

Oh My Mummies!
The Ins and Outs of MUMMIFICATION

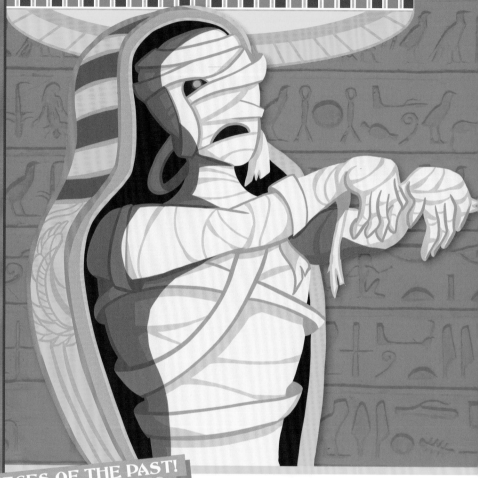

Just can't imagine life without your pet? The ancient Egyptians couldn't either. Some people even had mummies of their pets—from dogs and cats to birds and baboons—join them in their tomb. Bow-*wow*.

WHY MUMMIFY?

We know that the Egyptians believed in the afterlife—and that it wasn't always easy to get there. But the journey to the Land of the Dead could not start without one very important step: mummification. The Egyptians thought the soul would live on for all eternity only if the body was perfectly preserved. After all, if it decayed, your *Ba* and *Ka*—or your spirit—could not find their way back to you once you reached the afterlife.

THE *KA* AND THE *BA* OF IT ALL

According to the Egyptians, your soul split into two parts after you died, each part with a distinct form. One, the *Ka*, was a life force that later brought the dead back to life. It is what made the person alive.

The other part, the *Ba*, was the dead person's personality. Their sense of humor, compassion, and friendliness were all represented by the *Ba*. In ancient art, the *Ba* is represented by a bird with a human head. It was said to fly between the world of the living and the afterlife, so it could look after the dead's living family.

After a person died, the ancient Egyptians believed the *Ka* and *Ba* would leave the body and be reunited with it again in the afterlife. This is why it was so important for the body to be mummified: It needed to be whole and healthy for the soul to find its home again.

PERFECTLY PRESERVED

Egypt's dry desert air helped preserve a body from bacteria and decay. But it was still super important to prepare the body just right for burial. Throughout the ancient Egyptian civilization, mummification evolved and was perfected into a science and an art form. This careful precision and attention to detail made it possible for mummies to still exist today—thousands of years after their coffins were closed.

MUMMIFIED BY MISTAKE?

Experts think that the art of mummification may have happened by accident. Early on in the Egyptian civilization, bodies were buried in the desert because the fertile land near the Nile was needed for farming. The scorching sun and arid climate dried the bodies out and also prevented decay. After discovering the bodies still intact years later, Egyptians came up with a similar practice to preserve the dead.

NO-BRAINER

According to ancient Egyptians, everything about us—from our smarts to our sensitivity to all of our biological functions—was controlled by the heart. So when it came to the brain? They figured it had no real role. Later, science advanced and we learned that the brain is basically the control center of our bodies. But back then, the organ was considered useless— and embalmers threw it away!

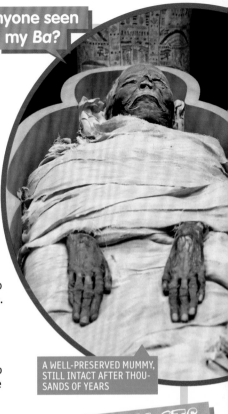

Anyone seen my *Ba*?

A WELL-PRESERVED MUMMY, STILL INTACT AFTER THOUSANDS OF YEARS

5 FREAKY FACTS ABOUT MUMMIES

1. Embalmers would sometimes place small onions or stones in the eye sockets to make the mummies appear to have eyes.

2. A 3,000-year-old mummy can still have fingerprints.

3. King Tut's embalmers used too much oil, which caused the mummy to carbonize, or turn into charcoal.

4. Sometimes bodies were stuffed with sawdust, plants, or linen to make them look more lifelike.

5. In the 1700s, artists painted with "mummy brown," a hue made from ground-up mummies.

Making a
Mummy

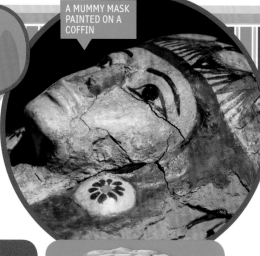

A MUMMY MASK PAINTED ON A COFFIN

Making a mummy was a highly specific job done by priests, and it usually took three months to complete the process. Here's how they did it back in the day.

1 The priests carefully washed the body, inside and out. Then, they rubbed it with scented oils and spices.

2 They removed the brain by pulling it out with a hook through the nose and tossed it.

3 They removed the liver, lungs, stomach, and intestines. These organs were stored in special pots, called canopic jars, to protect them from spells during the journey in the underworld. (Why didn't they touch the heart? Because the dead needed it to be judged in the afterlife.)

4 They sewed up any incisions made to remove the organs, and covered any cuts made into the flesh of the body.

5 They poured a special kind of powdery salt, called natron, all over the body. This dried it out and stalled decay. They next stuffed the body with scented rags to fill it out and make it look as lifelike as possible.

6 The priests said a prayer over the body, then left it for 40 days so it got nice and dry. They knew it was ready if the skin was tough like leather.

7 Time to beautify! The priests applied makeup to the face; clipped the fingernails and covered them with thin sheets of gold. Wigs or some yarn for hair were then added. You had to look good when facing your fate!

8 The body was wrapped in strips of linen dipped in resin, which hardened once dry. This process took about 20 layers, which equaled about a mile (1.6 km) of bandages! Good luck charms were stuck in different spots between the layers, thought to ward off evil spirits and protect the person in the afterlife.

9 A burial mask was placed over the head of the mummy. Since these resembled the person when he or she was living, the person's spirit would be able to recognize the body even after it was wrapped up.

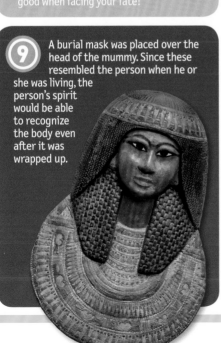

Afterlife, here I come!

10 The mummy went into its special case, painted to look like the person, with a copy of the *Book of the Dead* alongside the body. The person may have needed to reference it in the underworld.

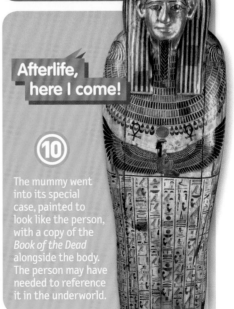

EGYPTOMANIA

Picture this: You're at a party, and someone decides to break out the games. But instead of divvying up into teams for charades or Monopoly, your host rolls out a mummy. The object of the game? To peel off the layers of linen to reveal the mummified body—and collect the valuable charms tucked away among the strips.

ALL ABOUT EGYPT. That may sound morbid, but back in the 1800s, plenty of Europeans unwrapped mummies for fun. In fact, more than 2,000 people attended one unwrapping party in London, England, in 1821. It was all part of Egyptomania, or the trend of obsessing over all things Egypt that spread across Europe after French military leader Napoleon Bonaparte invaded Egypt in the late 1700s. With a team of scientists and researchers that joined him on this expedition, Napoleon attempted to document what remained of ancient Egypt, which led to some major discoveries. Among them? The Rosetta Stone, which eventually helped Egyptologists crack the code of hieroglyphs—and revealed much of what we know about the ancient civilization today. (Read more about the Rosetta Stone on page 131!)

IN (NOT SO) LIVING COLOR. So how'd these folks get their hands on a mummy, anyway? After hearing about this fascinating land of pharaohs, some wealthier Europeans would travel to Egypt and bring them back as souvenirs! And they didn't just unwrap them: They'd display mummy parts in their living rooms as decor, just like you would a vase of flowers or a framed photo of your family.

THE CRAZE STAYS. While the mummy mania died down as the numbers of available wrapped-up remains dwindled, Egyptomania, in some form, remains as alive as ever. After all, if we weren't still fascinated by their culture, would you even be reading this book?

How OBSESSING Over Egypt Became a Worldwide PHENOMENON

DIG IT!
Some people would display mummy heads in glass domes around their homes!

Ancient Egyptian Funerals

Elaborate Ways Ancient Egyptians Said Their
FINAL FAREWELL

When it came to coffins, it was nothing but the finest for Egypt's pharaohs. Take King Tut's coffin—or make that *coffins*. The young king actually had *three* custom-made golden coffins, which fit inside each other like nesting dolls. The innermost coffin was solid gold and would be worth millions today. That's a lot of money to cough up for a coffin!

ALL ABOUT THE AFTERLIFE

Most pharaohs and important officials lived extravagant lives, so it makes total sense that their deaths would be just as over-the-top. The ceremony of saying goodbye to an ancient Egyptian VIP was an elaborate affair, complete with a procession, many mourners, and a banquet. The bigger the fanfare, the better his or her chances were to soar into the afterlife.

THE LONG HAUL

Once a royal's life ended, the funeral procession would begin. First, the body was placed into a plain coffin and taken by boat to the Valley of the Kings on the western bank of the Nile River. Once there, the coffin traveled to the Beautiful House, where priests would mummify the body and place it into a coffin, or mummy case. These coffins were often intricately decorated with images of the gods, as well as written spells meant to protect against the perils of the underworld.

After the mummification was complete, a long line of servants and mourners would follow the body in its coffin to the tomb site. They carried items important to the dead person, which would ultimately end up in the tomb to be used in the afterlife. This could include weapons, toys, instruments, food, drinks, and furniture. Tough luck if you got stuck carrying the heavy sofa!

SAD COMPANY

When it came to a final send-off, the more mourners, the merrier! Having a huge crowd at the funeral—and particularly the funeral procession—was a sign of just how beloved and respected the person was on Earth. The deceased's family sometimes even hired professional mourners to join the funeral procession and boost the numbers. But these people weren't paid just to walk along the route and look sad—they worked hard for their money! They'd scream, cry, and throw dust on themselves to show just how distraught they were about the death. Some tales tell of these wailing women beating their chests in agony and pulling out their hair in a spectacular show of grief to ensure that the deceased would reach the afterlife. Well, that's one way to do it.

OPEN WIDE

When the procession arrived at the tomb, the priest would say a prayer and conduct a special ceremony called the Opening of the Mouth. The coffin would be stood upright while the priest touched the mouth, eyes, and ears with a wand. This ritual was said to bring back the senses of the dead, allowing them to breathe, speak, eat, drink, move, and hear in the afterlife.

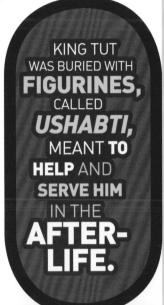

KING TUT WAS BURIED WITH **FIGURINES,** CALLED *USHABTI,* MEANT **TO HELP** AND **SERVE HIM** IN THE **AFTER-LIFE.**

Great Gods!
Ancient Egyptian MYTHOLOGY

ANCIENT ARTWORK SHOWS EGYPTIAN GODS BEING WORSHIPPED.

THERE'S A GOD FOR THAT!

In ancient Egypt, the gods ruled! The Egyptian religion was polytheistic—that is, Egyptians believed in many gods, or deities, who were thought to be in control of everything that happened in the world. They believed that each god had a specific job to do, from curing diseases to controlling the Nile's floods. Pharaohs—the mighty leaders of ancient Egypt—were believed to be directly connected to the gods, which made their status even more powerful. Because Egyptians were brought up to think that gods and goddesses watched over everything they did—and ultimately judged them after their death—they worked hard to please them so they'd be granted good health and good luck.

A LAND OF MANY MYTHS

The ancient Egyptians told a few different creation stories, which they wrote out in hieroglyphs found on pyramids, temples, tombs, and sheets of papyrus. The thing is, ancient Egypt was a big place—and the civilization lasted for a long, long time. Because the stories stem from varying regions and time frames, it's not surprising that many of these myths share different details about their deities. This can make mythology kind of confusing, like the fact that there are multiple sun gods, who go by lots of different names.

GREAT *EGG*-SPECTATIONS

One of the more common creation myths tells of an egg that appeared on the ocean during a time of dark chaos and nothingness, also known as Nun. When the egg hatched, out came the sun god, who coughed and spit out Shu, the god of air, and Tefnut, the goddess of moisture. Shu and Tefnut went on to have two children: Geb, the god of the Earth, and Nut, the goddess of the sky. Nut and Geb had four children, Osiris, Isis, Seth, and Nephthys, and together these gods made up the Ennead, or "the Nine," who are all credited as creators of the world.

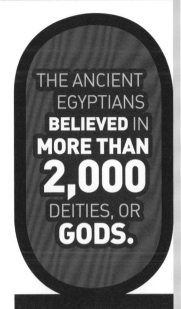

THE ANCIENT EGYPTIANS **BELIEVED** IN **MORE THAN 2,000** DEITIES, OR **GODS.**

Forecast: sunshine

Who's Who in the Nine
Everything You Need to Know About
THE ENNEAD

ATUM

ALSO KNOWN AS: One of the gods of the sun

WHY HE WAS WORSHIPPED: He was the reason the sun rose and set each day.

ODD DEITY DETAILS: Sometimes shown with the body of a man and the head of a falcon, Atum was credited for creating the world out of a watery nothingness. Egyptians thought he sailed across the sky every day in a golden boat.

SHU

ALSO KNOWN AS: God of air

WHY HE WAS WORSHIPPED: He would breathe life into all living creatures on Earth and provide gusts of wind that would power boats.

ODD DEITY DETAILS: Egyptians called clouds the "bones of Shu."

NEPHTHYS

ALSO KNOWN AS: Protector of the dead

WHY SHE WAS WORSHIPPED: She looked after the mummies and comforted the families of the deceased.

ODD DEITY DETAILS: A generous and kind goddess, Nephthys helped her sister, Isis, bring her husband, Osiris, back to life.

TEFNUT

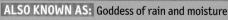

ALSO KNOWN AS: Goddess of rain and moisture

WHY SHE WAS WORSHIPPED: She brought the rainfall that the Egyptians needed to survive.

ODD DEITY DETAILS: It's said that when Tefnut grew angry with her father, Atum, she ran away and took all of Egypt's water with her, causing a drought.

SETH

ALSO KNOWN AS: God of the desert and chaos

WHY HE WAS WORSHIPPED: Ancient Egyptians mostly lived in fear of Seth, as they believed upsetting him would bring on hunger and thirst.

ODD DEITY DETAILS: Some myths say Seth would give the strength of a strong desert storm to anyone who worshipped him.

NUT

ALSO KNOWN AS: Goddess of the sky

WHY SHE WAS WORSHIPPED: She'd light up the sky with stars at night and keep order throughout Earth.

ODD DEITY DETAILS: The ancient Egyptians believed that each night, Nut swallowed the sun god and gave birth to him again the next morning.

OSIRIS

ALSO KNOWN AS: God of the dead and ruler of the afterlife

WHY HE WAS WORSHIPPED: Osiris made the final judgment of whether the dead was good enough for an eternal afterlife.

ODD DEITY DETAILS: Osiris is usually depicted with superdark green skin, said to symbolize the fertile soil of the Nile Valley.

GEB

ALSO KNOWN AS: God of the Earth

WHY HE WAS WORSHIPPED: He protected the sun and also accompanied the dead into the afterlife.

ODD DEITY DETAILS: Egyptians believed that Geb's laughter caused earthquakes.

ISIS

ALSO KNOWN AS: Goddess of magic and life

WHY SHE WAS WORSHIPPED: Like her husband, Osiris, she had the power of giving life after death.

ODD DEITY DETAILS: Seth killed Osiris by cutting him up into 42 pieces and throwing them into the Nile. Isis searched the world for his body parts and successfully put him back together using her magical spells.

Other Odd Gods

Of course, the Ennead weren't the only deities that the Egyptians believed in. There was a huge squad of gods they worshipped at home and in temples. Much like the ancient Greek gods, they were powerful and immortal. But they weren't portrayed as having bad tempers or drawn with human-like features, like Zeus and some of his crew were. Instead, many of the Egyptian gods were mostly peaceful—and had animal heads! Here are some of the main figures followed by the Egyptians.

BASTET

ALSO KNOWN AS: Goddess of the home

WHY SHE WAS WORSHIPPED: She protected all cats, which were sacred in ancient Egypt, as they were thought to chase off vermin from the crops.

ODD DEITY DETAILS:
The daughter of Atum, Bastet could harness the power of the sun to make crops grow. She appeared as a woman with a cat's head, giving her the modern nickname of the "cat goddess." Many bronze cat figures were created in her name.

HORUS

ALSO KNOWN AS:
God of kingship

WHY HE WAS WORSHIPPED:
He protected the pharaoh.

ODD DEITY DETAILS:
Some myths say his right eye was the sun and his left eye was the moon. He's said to bring protection, royal power, and good health.

BES

ALSO KNOWN AS: Protector against evil spirits and misfortune

WHY HE WAS WORSHIPPED: He brought happiness and peace.

ODD DEITY DETAILS: Part lion, part chubby man, Bes was cute, jolly, and protective. Myth says that he created loud music, which he played to celebrate the birth of a new baby—and to scare away any evil demons that might hurt the child.

ANUBIS

ALSO KNOWN AS: God of embalming

WHY HE WAS WORSHIPPED:
He protected mummies.

ODD DEITY DETAILS: Egyptians believed that Anubis, who had the head of a jackal—or wild dog—and the body of a man, watched over mummy making. To honor him, the chief priest wore a jackal mask while embalming a body.

WADJET

ALSO KNOWN AS: Protector of Lower Egypt

WHY SHE WAS WORSHIPPED: Often shown in cobra form, she protected her portion of Egypt, as well as the king.

ODD DEITY DETAILS: Wadjet kept a lookout on sacred spots. It's said she would punish robbers and criminals by blinding or poisoning them.

SEKHMET

ALSO KNOWN AS: Goddess of healing

WHY SHE WAS WORSHIPPED: She protected people from the plague and could cure disease.

ODD DEITY DETAILS: Born a vengeful killer, Sekhmet hatched a plan to wipe out the human race. Her concerned father stepped in by offering her a magical red drink she thought was blood. Turns out, the elixir made her forget about her awful act, and transformed her into a loving and pleasant goddess.

PTAH

ALSO KNOWN AS: God of craftsmen

WHY HE WAS WORSHIPPED: He was the creator of all things.

ODD DEITY DETAILS: Everything he wished for magically appeared. Some myths say Ptah, not Atum, created the world simply by imagining it and saying its name.

Sacred Spots
The Places Where People Could
WORSHIP THEIR FAVORITE GOD

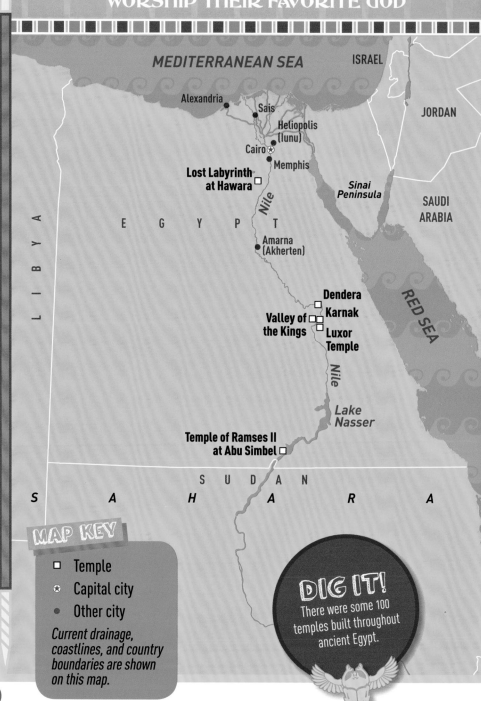

MEDITERRANEAN SEA

ISRAEL

JORDAN

Alexandria

Sais

Heliopolis
(Iunu)

Cairo ☆

Memphis

**Lost Labyrinth
at Hawara** □

Nile

*Sinai
Peninsula*

SAUDI
ARABIA

E   G   Y   P   T

**Amarna
(Akherten)**

L I B Y A

Dendera □
□ **Karnak**
Valley of □□
the Kings □ **Luxor
Temple**

RED SEA

Nile

*Lake
Nasser*

**Temple of Ramses II
at Abu Simbel** □

S   U   D   A   N

S   A   H   A   R   A

MAP KEY

□ Temple
☆ Capital city
● Other city

*Current drainage,
coastlines, and country
boundaries are shown
on this map.*

DIG IT!
There were some 100
temples built throughout
ancient Egypt.

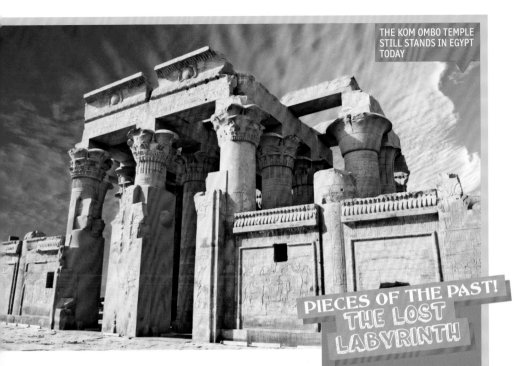

PIECES OF THE PAST!
THE LOST LABYRINTH

HOUSES FOR GODS

Sure, the ancient Egyptian gods weren't actual people. But that didn't stop the Egyptians from treating them like they were living and breathing beings! Some pharaohs oversaw the construction of giant stone temples that would hold larger-than-life statues of the gods. These statues were thought to be the earthly form of a god, and pharaohs and priests visited and cared for them as though they were beloved members of their families. The idea was that if the Egyptians took care of the gods in these sacred spots, the gods, in turn, would take care of them.

PRIVACY, PLEASE

The temples weren't just places of worship, like a church or a mosque. First off, they were huge—some the size of 200 soccer fields—to represent the giant presence of the gods. Also, they were totally private, with only the chief priest and the pharaoh allowed to enter the innermost shrine. There they'd watch over the statues and treat them like royalty. They'd play music, burn incense, and do other tasks to please the deity. Once or twice a year, the priest would carry a statue outside for festivals, so ordinary people would get to bask in the glow of their favorite god (flip to page 114 for more fun facts about festivals).

Its walls are covered in hieroglyphs, there are 3,000 secret chambers, a maze of passages, a dozen palaces, and final resting spots for sacred crocodiles. It just may be the biggest temple ever built by the ancient Egyptians—yet no one has actually ever seen it. Why? Because this massive sacred spot—also known as the Lost Labyrinth—is likely buried 16 feet (5 m) beneath the sand in Hawara, about 56 miles (90 km) south of Cairo. First written about some 2,500 years ago by ancient historian Herodotus, the labyrinth was described as a "work beyond words" and massive enough to hold the great temples of Karnak and Luxor. While recent studies using high-tech scans of the ground showed that there is likely a large temple hidden below the sand, the Egyptian government is keeping the area off-limits to archaeologists. So for now, the truth about the Lost Labyrinth remains, well, buried.

109

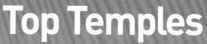

Top Temples
Wow-worthy PLACES OF WORSHIP

LUXOR

BUILT: About 3,400 years ago by Amenhotep III, with other pharaohs, like Ramses II, later adding to it.

THE GODS: One of the sun gods, Amun, mother goddess Mut, and Khonsu, god of the moon

FUNKY FACTS: Pharaoh Ramses II made sure to put huge statues of himself at the entrance of Luxor, so he'd always be the first to greet his favorite god when he arrived for the annual Opet festival.

ABU SIMBEL

BUILT: About 3,300 years ago by Ramses II.

THE GODS: Sun gods Amun and Re-Horakhty, plus Ptah, god of craftsmen

FUNKY FACTS: This temple is marked by four colossal statues of Ramses II at the main entrance, each as tall as a six-story building. Twice a year, the first rays of the morning sun flood the whole length of the temple, illuminating even its innermost sanctuary.

DENDERA

BUILT: Parts of the complex were constructed about 4,000 years ago by Pepi I.

THE GOD: Hathor, goddess of love

FUNKY FACTS: The temple features a ceiling painted like the night sky. A place of healing, sick people seeking cures would travel to Dendera. There, they'd stay in special housing near the temple, where they could rest and chat with the gods in their dreams.

KARNAK

BUILT: Completed about 2,000 years ago by Amenhotep I, but some parts date back to much earlier than that.

THE GODS: Sun god Amun, mother goddess Mut, and Khonsu, god of the moon

FUNKY FACTS: Three temples in one, Karnak is the largest religious complex in Egypt. Its great temple, known as Hypostyle Hall, is big enough to hold Paris' Notre Dame Cathedral!

SPOILED STATUES!

Back in ancient Egypt, the gods lived the good life! Priests would feed their sacred statues three meals a day, featuring fancy foods like meat, fruit, veggies, and bread. They'd also sprinkle them with water from a sacred lake and douse them with perfume. Because who wants a smelly statue?

RESEARCHERS RECENTLY DISCOVERED A **2,000-YEAR-OLD SPHINX** WHILE DOING WORK ON AN **EGYPTIAN TEMPLE.**

9 Cool Things About
The Great Sphinx

It's one of the most iconic structures in Egypt: a giant statue with the head of a pharaoh and the body of a lion looming large over the Nile River near six pyramids. This is the Great Sphinx of Giza, and it is as tall as the White House in Washington, D.C., with paws longer than a city bus. But what's the story behind this supersize statue? Dig into these details about the mystical monument.

1 ON GUARD

The mythical mash-up of a human and a lion was worshipped in ancient Egypt for its power to ward off evil. Some think the Sphinx was built to protect the pyramids—and the pharaohs who were buried inside.

2 NAME GAME

What's in a name? The name "Sphinx" actually comes from the ancient Greeks: The Egyptians originally called it *Hor-em-akhet*, a nod to Horus, the god of the sky. It was also referred to in Egyptian as *shesep ankh*, which meant "living image."

3 SET IN STONE

Instead of being assembled piece by piece like the pyramids, the Sphinx was carved from a single mass of limestone. At more than six stories tall and about half as long as a city block, that was one colossal chunk of stone.

4 ANCIENT ORIGINS

Nobody's sure when the Sphinx was built. Studies show that it likely dates back to the time of the Old Kingdom between the years 2558 and 2532 B.C. Experts believe it was already ancient when Egyptian queen Cleopatra laid eyes on it around 47 B.C.

Oooo, an antique

DIG IT!
The Great Sphinx
weighs more than 50,747
jumbo jets.

⑤ WORK OF KINGS

Who built the Great Sphinx is also a mystery, although experts have narrowed it down to either Pharaoh Khufu or his son, Pharaoh Khafre. The Sphinx's face looks like sculptures made of both of the men, and a temple that sits in front of the statue seems to be the work of Khafre.

STATUE OF KHAFRE

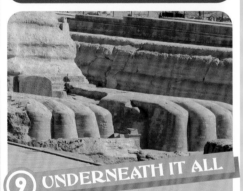

⑥ CLEAN SHAVE

The Sphinx originally sported a beard, which crumbled after centuries of wind and rain ground away at the statue's limestone. A piece of its "stubble" is on display at London's British Museum.

⑦ BURIED IN SAND

For thousands of years, the Sphinx was buried up to its shoulders in sand, which had accumulated over the years. It wasn't until 1817 that the first wave of archaeologists began to dig out the Sphinx.

⑨ UNDERNEATH IT ALL

Legend says the library of the sunken island of Atlantis is buried beneath the Sphinx, with an entrance near its right paw. Nothing has ever been found to support this theory, but experts did find an ancient settlement larger than 10 football fields hidden near the Sphinx: This lost city is thought to have been the home of workers who built the pyramids and the Sphinx some 4,500 years ago.

⑧ SEEING RED

The Sphinx may be sand-colored today, but traces of pigment found on the limestone statue show that it was once painted bright red, yellow, and blue.

113

Celebrating the Gods!
Ancient Egyptian Festivals HONORING THEIR SACRED DEITIES

A PHARAOH LEADS A FESTIVAL PROCESSION.

PRAISE AND PARTY TIME

No doubt, everyone in ancient Egypt worked very hard. But they played hard, too. In fact, the civilization took part in hundreds of festivals every year, and most of them centered around celebrating the gods. These public parties—sometimes lasting for three weeks—had tons of food, music, and dancing. They were a chance for the Egyptians to show off their dedication to the deities, whom they believed controlled everything in their lives, down to the weather.

ALL EYES ON AMUN

Each year, crowds gathered outside the Luxor Temple—each individual hoping to have a brush with greatness both outside and inside the shrine. But it wasn't an Egyptian celebrity they were seeking to rub elbows with. Rather, these common folk clamored to get a glimpse of the sacred statue of the god Amun, the creator god, and widely known as the King of the Gods.

The annual procession, known as the Opet festival, saw Amun's statue transported from Karnak to Luxor—a 1.5-mile (2.4-km) journey. The statue, which was dressed in fine linen, doused in perfume, and accessorized with gold jewelry, would be carried on the shoulders of priests through the crowded streets. Music played, and priests would sing as they shuttled the statue.

THE CROWD GOES WILD

After arriving at Luxor, the pharaoh and his priests entered the temple and performed a private ceremony to pray for the god's blessings on their land and harvest. Then the pharaoh would emerge to an adoring crowd pumped by the potential of being in the presence of royalty and a great god. Adding to the excitement? The crowds would receive handouts of loaves of bread and sweets.

TALKING WALLS

The Opet festival also allowed the very rare chance of entering the temple to "talk" to the god. Except that Amun wasn't big on chitchat. Instead, when a person asked the god a question, a priest—speaking from a secret spot within the temple's walls—would answer. Sneaky, sneaky!

FLIPPING OUT

Ancient Egyptians also lived it up with parties marking big events in life, like the annual harvest, the birth of a baby, and even the death of a loved one (after all, sending someone off to the afterlife was a big deal worth celebrating!). Ancient tomb paintings reveal scenes of people partying it up at banquets with buffets of food, music, dancing, and even entertainment by acrobats, who'd tumble and twist for guests. Now that's one way to make people *flip* for your parties!

Where's the party?

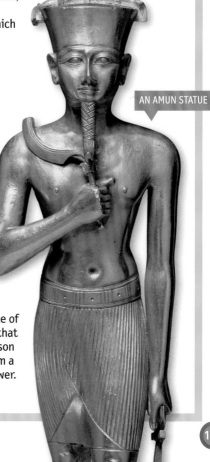

AN AMUN STATUE

4 Other Fabulous Festivals

① FESTIVAL OF BAST

ALSO KNOWN AS: Festival of Cats

FESTIVAL FACTS: *Meow!* This day was all about felines. The festival honored Bastet, the goddess of cats, and was marked by dancing, music-making, and merriment. Thousands of people would flock to the Temple of Bastet for the festival to celebrate this cat-tastic day.

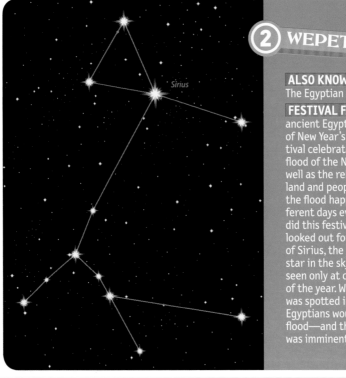

Sirius

② WEPET RENPET

ALSO KNOWN AS: The Egyptian New Year

FESTIVAL FACTS: The ancient Egyptians' version of New Year's Day, this festival celebrated the annual flood of the Nile River—as well as the rebirth of the land and people. Because the flood happened on different days every year, so did this festival. Egyptians looked out for the return of Sirius, the brightest star in the sky, which is seen only at certain times of the year. When Sirius was spotted in the sky, the Egyptians would know the flood—and the festival—was imminent.

③ HEB-SED FESTIVAL

ALSO KNOWN AS: Feast of the Tail

FESTIVAL FACTS: The ancient Egyptians believed that their pharaoh was the most powerful being on Earth, but even the king needed a bit of a divine boost once in a while. So 30 years into a pharaoh's reign, he'd be "revitalized" by the gods with this festival. People watched as the pharaoh first offered gifts to the gods. The pharaoh would then attach a bull's tail to his or her robe and run around an enclosed course four times to show his or her renewed fitness—injected into him by the gods. Sometimes, the pharaoh would fire arrows into the sky as a show of dominance over all of the land. The festival would repeat every three years from that point on until a new pharaoh came to power.

④ WAG FESTIVAL

ALSO KNOWN AS: Day of the Dead

FESTIVAL FACTS: One of the oldest festivals celebrated by the Egyptians, this gathering honored the souls of the dead on their journey to the afterlife. To mark the occasion, there'd be nighttime, torch-lit processions to statues outside of temples, where people would leave offerings, like bread and cakes.

SOME **70,000 PEOPLE** WERE SAID TO HAVE ATTENDED **ONE FESTIVAL** HONORING THE **GODDESS BASTET.**

Animal Idols
Meet the CREATURES
Egyptians Believed Were LIVING GODS

CHERISHED CREATURES

Don't cross that cat! In ancient Egypt, certain animals were treated far better than the average pet. That's because they were seen as vessels for the spirits of the gods. Religious groups known as cults would worship specific animals, including types of fish, birds, reptiles, and mammals. Sanctuaries were built for these cherished creatures, their bodies would be mummified and buried in tombs, and people would wear certain items representing the animals, like amulets, to keep them close—and to keep the gods pleased.

FANCY FELINES

Sure, cats are said to have nine lives. But in ancient Egypt, they lived double lives, too. How? They were praised as pets *and* as a supernatural species. So around the house, the kitties would probably catch mice and snooze in the sunlight just like your pet may do. But throughout the society, cats were admired for their connection to the gods and honored through artwork, like statues and sculptures. (It's no wonder, then, that the penalty for killing a cat—even accidentally—was death. Yikes!)

EGYPTIANS WERE KNOWN TO **MUMMIFY SCARAB BEETLES**— AND THEIR **POOP!**

BIG-TIME BULL

One of the most popular animal stories in ancient Egypt was centered around the Apis bull. The story goes that Ptah, the god of craftsmen, had a magical, fortune-telling bull with very specific markings, including a triangle-shaped tuft of white hair on its otherwise all-black hide, plus a black-and-white tail.

In real life, ancient Egyptians would put on a nationwide search for a calf born with similar markings. And when one was? They'd give that babe the royal treatment, keep it in a special sanctuary, adorned with gold and jewels, pampered by priests, and visited by people from all over Egypt. There was only one Apis bull at a time, and when it passed away, it would be mummified, laid to rest in a lavish ceremony, and mourned throughout the country before a replacement calf was sought out—and eventually brought to the capital city on a custom-built boat.

GOOD LUCK BUG

For such a little critter, the scarab beetle made a huge impression on Egyptians. This insect—also known as the dung beetle because of its habit of rolling animal poop into big balls before either eating it or laying eggs in it—appears everywhere throughout ancient Egyptian history. The scarab's rolling actions reminded the Egyptians of the sun rolling up out of the horizon at dawn. So they connected the beetle to the sun god.

For good luck in the afterlife, embalmers would place scarab-shaped amulets within the layers of bandages on a mummy, and women would wear jewelry decorated with the image of the beetle. In fact, hundreds of thousands of these artifacts have been excavated in Egypt, proving just how much influence this insect had.

MONKEY BUSINESS

Monkeys weren't native to Egypt, but that didn't stop thousands of people from praising the primates. Brought to the shores of the Nile from other regions in Africa through trade by merchants, monkeys soon became sacred because of their connection to the gods. The Egyptians saw baboons, specifically, as living links to Thoth, the god of the moon, magic, and wisdom, and kept them in temples, where they were cared for by priests. Some monkeys were also kept by police, who would train them to help on patrol.

DIG IT!
After the death of the worshipped Apis bull, people would shave their heads and mourn for 60 days.

PIECES OF THE PAST!
LION AROUND

Ancient Egyptians were just wild about lions! Thought to have divine powers, these big cats were symbols of strength throughout ancient Egypt. Statues of lions even guarded the country's borders, as well as the pharaoh's chariot and throne. But the cats cast a powerful presence in real life, too. Lions were bred and raised in sanctuaries throughout ancient Egypt. And in 2004, a team of French archaeologists unearthed the first mummified lion ever found in an Egyptian tomb. They found a complete skeleton of a male lion, who likely died of old age, on a rock surrounded by other animal bones within the tomb of one of King Tut's caretakers. Experts say that the remarkable preservation and careful placement within the tomb proved that lions indeed had sacred status in Egypt.

10 Facts About the
VIPs* of Ancient Egypt
(*Very Important Pets)

Sacred animals weren't the only creatures Egyptians kept their eyes on—they had pets, too! In fact, the Egyptians were one of the first civilizations to keep animals around the house, and during the New Kingdom, almost every household had a pet. Here's more about the prized pets of ancient Egypt.

Who needs eyebrows?

① FAVORITE FELINES

The Egyptians loved their pet cats so much that when one died, it's said that they'd shave their eyebrows in mourning.

② SHORT LEASH

A wall painting dating back some 4,500 years shows a man taking his dog for a walk on a leash.

③ MANE MAN

King Ramses II had a pet lion named Slayer of His Enemies.

④ MONKEYING AROUND

Archaeologists recently discovered a cemetery dating back 2,000 years, containing the graves of some 100 animals, including a monkey wearing an iron collar.

⑤ NAME GAME

Miit—the Egyptian word for cat—was a popular name for girls.

⑥ ROYAL TREATMENT

Prince Thutmose, King Amenhotep III's son, buried his pet cat in its own stone sarcophagus.

⑦ A BEAST'S FEAST

Some pet crocodiles ate better than most people, with a diet of high-quality meats and honey cakes.

⑧ ON THE HUNT

Some Egyptians kept pet mongooses, most likely to tag along on hunting trips.

⑨ OLD BREED

The basenji—a breed of dog still seen today—was a popular pet and guard dog throughout ancient Egypt.

⑩ GREAT GAZELLE

One Egyptian noblewoman ordered a custom-made coffin for her pet gazelle, which was mummified and later placed in her tomb when she died.

All About Art
Brushing Up on
ANCIENT EGYPTIAN ARTWORK

AN EGYPTIAN WALL PAINTING FROM QUEEN NEFERTARI'S TOMB

DIG IT!
In ancient art, women often had light red or yellow skin while the men's was reddish brown.

MORE THAN JUST A PRETTY PICTURE

Egyptian art wasn't just pretty to look at: There was a ton of symbolism in it, too. These works of art told stories of people's lives, great battles, the gods they worshipped, and more. From paintings to pottery and carvings to columns, ancient Egyptians left behind a collection of creations, many of which have managed to stand the test of time. And because this ancient artwork was built to last, experts have been able to study these illustrations and etchings to get a better glimpse of just what was going on in the world back then.

ROCKING RESOURCES

Just how has this ancient art hung around for so long? The combination of the durable materials used in ancient Egyptian art—like stone and clay—and the dry desert air created the perfect conditions for preservation. Artists of the Egyptian civilization were also super resourceful: From carving statues out of rock in desert cliffs to slicing papyrus stalks into strips and sticking them together to form a durable canvas, the Egyptians made full use of what they had on hand.

NOTHING TO SEE HERE

Most ancient Egyptian art that we can look at now was never meant to see the light of day—literally. Egyptians filled the tombs of pharaohs and other important people with this art, which was meant to help protect the dead during their journey into the afterlife, or simply as comfort for the deceased. It wasn't until modern explorers discovered the ancient tombs—and all the artwork—that pieces were brought to the surface and, eventually, ended up in museums around the world.

PIECES OF THE PAST! (VERY) OLD ART

Just how well did the dry desert help to preserve ancient art? Well enough to keep some rock carvings intact for 15,000 years! Rock carvings chiseled into sandstone cliffs in the village of Qurta—about 400 miles (640 km) south of Cairo—are considered among the oldest works of art on Earth. The images—many of them featuring a now-extinct cow with horns—are as impressive in size as they are in age. Experts have discovered panels of artwork measuring more than a mile (1.6 km) long!

EGYPT WAS THE **ONLY ANCIENT** CIVILIZATION ABLE TO **PRODUCE BLUE DYES**— AND THE FIRST TO HAVE A **WORD FOR BLUE**.

COLORFUL WORKS OF ANCIENT ART

True Colors!

Standout Shades in ANCIENT EGYPTIAN ART

One of the most amazing attributes of Egyptian art is its brilliant colors. From bold hues in murals to brilliant tones in wall paintings, color was important and had specific symbolism. Each color held a special meaning and was chosen to show a certain feeling or idea.

GREEN

THE SYMBOLISM: New life, joy, growth, and positivity

ARTSY EXAMPLE: Ancient Egypt's heavenly afterlife—also known as the Field of Reeds—was often painted in green.

DID *HUE* KNOW? In ancient Egypt, to do "green things" was another way to say one was living in a positive way.

WHITE

THE SYMBOLISM: Purity, cleanliness, and power

ARTSY EXAMPLE: Sacred animals, like cows and oxen, would appear in white.

DID *HUE* KNOW? The floors of temples were made of white limestone.

How'd they get that hue? To make paint, ancient Egyptians used minerals dug up from the ground. Certain components, including carbon, iron, azurite, and malachite, would be mixed together with other organic material and a sticky, shiny substance, like egg whites or beeswax, to create different colors of paint that would adhere to all sorts of surfaces. And it definitely, well, *stuck*: The walls of tombs dating back at least 3,200 years still boast bold colors as though they were painted mere decades ago.

BLACK

THE SYMBOLISM: Death and night

ARTSY EXAMPLE: Anubis, the god of the dead and embalming, had a black jackal's head and a human's body.

DID *HUE* KNOW? Ancient Egyptians would sometimes create black dyes from the soot of burned animal bones.

GOLD

THE SYMBOLISM: Eternal life and the sun

ARTSY EXAMPLE: Each god's skin was shaded with gold to underscore their immortality.

DID *HUE* KNOW? Mummies were given a golden amulet, or charm, for protection—and to ensure they'd live as long as the sun shone.

BLUE

THE SYMBOLISM: Water, the sky, birth, rebirth, and life

ARTSY EXAMPLE: A small sculpture of a blue hippo was found in the tomb of an Egyptian nobleman, likely put there so that the deceased could control the Nile in the afterlife.

DID *HUE* KNOW? Some women would get blue symbols tattooed on their bodies to protect them during pregnancy and childbirth.

RED

THE SYMBOLISM: Life, victory, anger, and chaos

ARTSY EXAMPLE: The murderous god Seth (remember, he killed his brother?) had red eyes and hair.

DID *HUE* KNOW? In writing, scribes switched from black ink to red when they wrote the word "evil."

IT'S IN THE DETAILS!

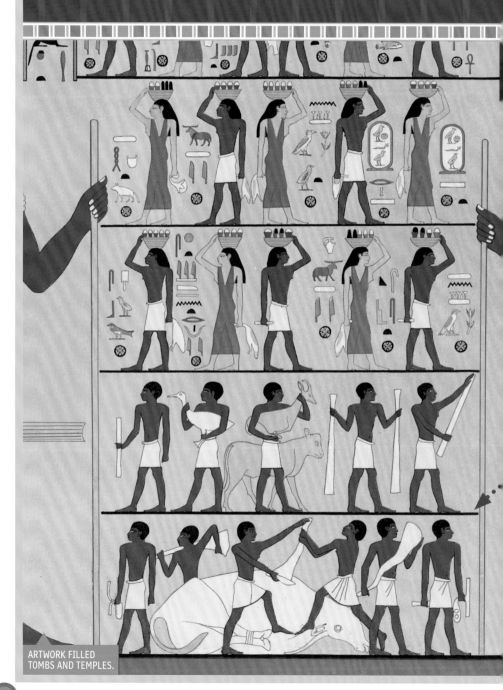

ARTWORK FILLED TOMBS AND TEMPLES.

WAYS IN WHICH Egyptian Art Was Super Unique FOR ITS TIME

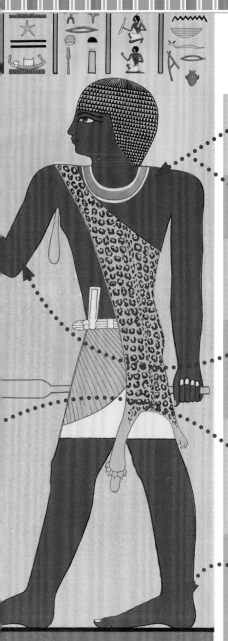

Egyptian art had a look all its own! Its unique features, especially the way people are depicted, makes it one of the most recognizable styles of art of all time.

SIDE SHOW. Faces, waists, and limbs were also shown in profile, while eyes and shoulders were shown in frontal view.

UP RIGHT. People usually sit or stand in a stiff and formal posture.

FLAT FEATURES. Egyptian art is very flat. There is no horizon or depth.

BIG SHOT. A person appearing bigger than others in a painting was meant to show his or her importance. Pharaohs, for example, were usually drawn larger than the average Egyptian.

KEEPING ORDER. Parallel lines, called registers, were used to create order and to separate scenes in a painting. Examples of art that don't have registers were usually battle or hunting scenes—a lack of a register symbolized chaos.

WALK LIKE AN EGYPTIAN. People's feet were always shown sideways. This makes each individual foot more distinguishable than if they were shown head-on and also gives the figures a sense of formality and establishes a sense of balance.

A REAL WORK OF ART?

It is a painting praised for its level of detail and simple beauty. People have even compared it to Leonardo da Vinci's "Mona Lisa," arguably the most recognized painting in the world. But now, this so-called masterpiece is famous for another reason: Some experts think it may be a fake. Here's more about the, uh, wild goose chase to uncover the truth about this painting.

ALSO KNOWN AS "MEIDUM GEESE,"

this image of three pairs of geese was supposedly plucked from the Meidum pyramid, built by Pharaoh Snefru some 4,500 years ago. The story goes that an Italian scholar, artist, and Egyptologist named Luigi Vassalli discovered it in 1871 in the tomb of Snefru's daughter-in-law, Atet, and put it on display in a museum. It has been celebrated and admired ever since for its high level of quality and balance.

ARCHAEOLOGIST FRANCESCO TIRADRITTI

has made a shocking claim about the painting: He says it's not from ancient Egypt, but is perhaps a much more modern masterpiece. Tiradritti studied the actual painting, as well as high-res photographs, to come up with his conclusion.

METHODS BEHIND THE MASTERPIECE

Using high-tech scanning technology, scientists recently revealed just what kind of paint and tools ancient Egyptians used to craft their portraits. After studying scans of an 1,800-year-old portrait of a woman through a superpowered magnifying lens, the scientists were able to pick out details invisible to the naked eye. For instance, they could tell that the paint was made from plant dyes and bonded by beeswax. They also examined the brush strokes on the canvas to determine that the artist used different tools to paint the portrait—which was attached to the mummy of a noblewoman living in the second century A.D.— including a fine brush, a metal spoon, and an engraver.

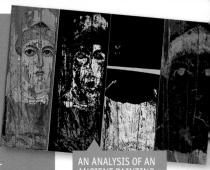

AN ANALYSIS OF AN ANCIENT PAINTING REVEALS THE TOOLS THE ARTIST USED.

THE MYSTERY of Ancient Egypt's "MONA LISA"

ONE OF TIRADRITTI'S CLAIMS IS that the type of geese in the painting would probably never have flown south to Egypt. The bean goose and the red-breasted goose tend to live in much colder climates and likely would not have ever existed in Egypt.

TIRADRITTI ALSO SAYS THAT the painting features shades of red and orange that aren't consistent with other ancient Egyptian artwork. There's also no beige in the work, a color that pops up in plenty of other art of the time.

PAINTING THE TRUTH. Tiradritti's theory? That Vassalli himself painted the "Meidum Geese" over another painting— perhaps a less-impressive image he did find in the pyramid. While we may never get the whole picture surrounding this painting, Tiradritti's claim is a reminder that when it comes to "ancient" art, there may be more to it than meets the eye.

PIECES OF THE PAST! ANIMALS IN ART

The ancient Egyptians were wild about wildlife! They'd include images of all sorts of animals in their artwork, from hunting scenes drawn on the walls of Egyptian tombs to reliefs. Besides sacred animals, like crocs and cats, they would also feature creatures that were important to their daily lives, like cows and horses. Or they'd include animals to show what was going on around them, like hopping frogs and soaring dragonflies in scenes of people fishing in the Nile River.

Wildlife is so common in ancient Egyptian art that scientists have actually studied it to determine how animals have evolved—and when certain species went extinct—based on when they stopped appearing in images. For example, in early paintings, you'd see rhinos, antelopes, and giraffes, which stopped showing up in later images. Experts think these animals may have disappeared around the same time due to hunting or the shift in Egypt's climate. Just goes to show we can learn a lot from art.

It Is Written!
HIEROGLYPHS—One of Egypt's HARDEST MYSTERIES to Decode

THE **ANCIENT EGYPTIAN LANGUAGE** USES MORE THAN **3,100** HIEROGLYPHS.

SO MANY SYMBOLS!

Imagine if our alphabet was made of pictures and symbols instead of letters. Reading and writing would be awfully tricky, huh? That's what the ancient Egyptians had to work with through their complex system of symbols, also known as hieroglyphs. The world's first known form of written communication, hieroglyphs were the way that the ancient Egyptians shared their stories and recorded their history. They are not quite an alphabet like we know. Instead, they focus on sounds or represent a whole syllable or even an entire word.

MYSTERIOUS SCRIPT

Hieroglyphs can be found pretty much everywhere in ancient Egypt. They were etched into tomb walls, written on statues, and recorded on long papyrus scrolls. But trying to decipher what these pictures mean and how they translate to our language is a tricky task. So it's no wonder that until the 19th century, no one in the modern world could figure out what these mystical symbols were actually saying.

CRACKING THE CODE

Picture this: You find an ancient block of rock covered in mysterious symbols. Your job? To figure out what these symbols mean, in the hopes of unlocking centuries of secrets tucked away in ancient Egypt's history.

That's just what happened to a pair of European language experts when they got their hands on the Rosetta Stone, a 3.5-foot (1-m)-tall block of granodiorite (a granite-like rock) covered in hieroglyphs. The stone—also known as a stela—was dug up in 1799 during the French invasion of Egypt and eventually brought to Thomas Young of England and Jean-François Champollion of France in the hopes that they'd crack the code.

IN THE LOOP

And that they did: But it took some time. Fourteen years, to be exact! First, Young realized that some symbols were circled by an oval loop. Later defined as a cartouche, this is the way pharaohs' names were presented in hieroglyphs. But Young didn't know that … yet. So he took note of the loops and moved along.

IT'S ALL GREEK!

Later, Champollion observed that in addition to hieroglyphs, the words were also etched in Greek (the stone dated back to the time when Greek-speaking kings ruled over Egypt). Because Champollion understood Greek, he could translate the symbols and compare each hieroglyph to the Greek translation. This led to Champollion's epic *aha* moment: Each symbol represented a sound.

FULL CIRCLE

Now, let's go back to those loops. In 1822, Champollion deciphered the name of a king, Ptolemy V, within a cartouche. He also made some smart matches, like linking the sun symbol to the Egyptian word "ra," one of the Egyptians' names for their sun god. From there, Champollion translated everything on the Rosetta Stone. And though Champollion made the final connection, both men's efforts contributed to this crucial discovery that ultimately led to revealing almost everything we now know about ancient Egypt. Talk about teamwork!

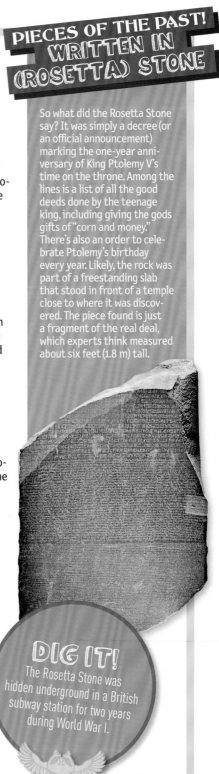

So what did the Rosetta Stone say? It was simply a decree (or an official announcement) marking the one-year anniversary of King Ptolemy V's time on the throne. Among the lines is a list of all the good deeds done by the teenage king, including giving the gods gifts of "corn and money." There's also an order to celebrate Ptolemy's birthday every year. Likely, the rock was part of a freestanding slab that stood in front of a temple close to where it was discovered. The piece found is just a fragment of the real deal, which experts think measured about six feet (1.8 m) tall.

DIG IT!

The Rosetta Stone was hidden underground in a British subway station for two years during World War I.

Write On!

The IMPORTANT ROLES SCRIBES Played in Ancient Egypt

A COVETED CAREER

Scribes sure had big jobs to do! As the people who recorded everything that went on in ancient Egypt—from laws and statistics to songs and religious texts—their work was super important in keeping order throughout the civilization. Not just anyone could become a scribe. It took special schooling and tons of smarts, which made it quite a coveted career.

OFF TO SCHOOL ... FOREVER

At a young age, some kids—typically the children of scribes—would start scribal school, usually located within a temple. There they'd study the hundreds of hieroglyphs and memorize them all. To learn them, the students would copy the symbols over and over onto sheets of papyrus, or old pieces of pottery, or on smooth wood. Committing thousands of symbols to memory took plenty of time—and practice: It could take a student up to 12 years to complete scribal school!

ON THE JOB

Newly minted scribes were sent throughout the country to document everything—even detailed directions for how to perform brain surgery! Scribes would be assigned to a certain person or area and sit, cross-legged, with a wooden board on their lap to write down everything they'd observe. Sometimes, scribes were given more simple tasks, like writing letters for people who didn't know how, or keeping track of supplies in the temples. The more experience they gained, the higher they would rise—and for some, that was all the way to the top-ranking position of royal scribe. This powerful position placed scribes at the right hand of a pharaoh to advise the leader, design the writings that would go on temples and tombs, and even do more trivial tasks like writing poems for the royal family.

PERKS OF THE JOB

Because the scribes were treated really well, the positions were sought after. Unlike commoners, scribes were exempt from paying taxes, and they didn't have to be in the military or do manual labor. If a scribe rose in the ranks and became a royal scribe, he or she would be paid handsomely and given land to boot. Having a direct link to the pharaoh—and an insider's access into the royal palace—made this position among the most powerful throughout ancient Egyptian society.

A LOOK INSIDE A ROYAL SCRIBE'S TOMB

The recent discovery of a tomb of a royal scribe is shedding new light into the life of these ancient officials. The 3,000-year-old tomb—likely belonging to a scribe named Khonsu, who served Amenhotep III, King Tut's grandfather—was unearthed by a team of Japanese archaeologists in ancient Thebes, near the Valley of the Kings. About the size of a large bedroom in your house (pretty big by tomb standards), the space is decorated with colorful paintings showing the scribe in different scenes, like worshipping the gods Osiris and Isis with his wife. There are also carvings of baboons worshipping the sun god, which may be a nod to Khonsu's favorite animal. Such careful attention to personal detail, experts say, is a sign showing just how respected scribes were back in the day.

TOOLS OF THE TRADE

A scribe never left home without ...

- A roll of papyrus
- A pen made from a thin reed and topped with a small brush
- A wooden palette for ink with two impressions (one spot for black, one spot for red)

A SCRIBE AT WORK

A Royal Place to Learn
Cracking the Book on Ancient Egypt's
LIBRARY OF ALEXANDRIA

BY THE BOOKS

There are a lot of downsides to being invaded by another country. But after Alexander the Great took control of Egypt, the Greeks left a rather significant memento behind: The Royal Library of Alexandria. It is considered the most famous ancient library in the world. People, including famous scholars, would flock to it from near and far to study and learn there.

STAY HERE, LEARN HERE

The shelves of the Royal Library weren't filled with books as we know them, though. Back then, things were often written on papyrus scrolls. The library's collection was made up of some 500,000 scrolls containing info about math, science, literature, history, and law, plus works from some of the greatest thinkers of the time, like Homer, Plato, and Socrates. Like a college campus, the Royal Library had places to stay, dining halls, labs, observatories, gardens, and even a zoo. The place was bustling with brainiacs eager to learn at this educational epicenter.

COPY THAT

The Royal Library got its texts in a pretty unusual way. First, after ships carrying the scrolls arrived in Alexandria, scribes took them from the sailors and would quickly copy the entire scroll by hand. The scribes would then return the original copy of the text to the sailors and file the duplicate scroll on the shelves. Sounds like they could've used a copy machine!

PROTECTING THE BOOKS

In 2011, Egypt was embroiled in an 18-day political revolution that ultimately led to the resignation of then-president Hosni Mubarak. And, once again, the newly built Royal Library was at the center of the turmoil. But history did not repeat itself. Determined to protect their beloved place of learning, the people of Alexandria went into action. Hundreds of people joined hands and formed a human chain around the library, chanting "We love you Egypt," as they kept the crowds away. The tactic worked—and the library remains a popular spot in Alexandria today.

A MYSTERIOUS ENDING

While most experts agree that the Royal Library was a remarkable place, what happened to it remains somewhat of a mystery. What we do know is that the library did burn to the ground at some point. The likeliest story is that the library caught fire during Julius Caesar's attack on Egypt in 48 B.C. Other theories are that it was burned during battle, perhaps after the Muslim conquest of Alexandria in A.D. 641.

ROYAL LIBRARY 2.0

It may have taken thousands of years, but in 2002, the Royal Library reappeared in Alexandria. This time, it was a gleaming, state-of-the-art center containing rare, ancient texts, high-tech computers, and a science museum. Costing more than $200 million, the library was built with one very important feature in mind: It's virtually fireproof.

School Rules!
EDUCATION in Ancient Egypt

Zzzz

A TRIO OF SCRIBES TAKING NOTES IN CLASS

THE ANCIENT EGYPTIAN **SCHOOL DAY** USUALLY INCLUDED AN **AFTERNOON NAP** TO BEAT THE DESERT **HEAT.**

THEY'VE GOT CLASS

Believe it or not, school hasn't changed *all* that much since the days of ancient Egypt. Back then, there were teachers (who were usually strict), rows of desks or tables, and even lists of rules posted on the walls. Sound familiar? The main difference between now and then was that school wasn't open to everyone like it is now. In fact, back then, only kids from the wealthiest families would get a formal education—and in most cases, classes were filled with boys only. General schools were built in almost every village, but the supersmart—or superconnected—kids would go off to scribal school. Still, only a small portion of Egyptians got a formal education.

SCHOOL DAY SCHEDULE

If you were a well-off 10-year-old kid in ancient Egypt, your day would go a little like this: Wake up, eat breakfast, and head to school. Once there, you'd sit at a table and start your studies in a variety of subjects, including geography, reading, writing, religion, math, morals, and ethics. You'd read texts aloud and work to memorize them.

Around noon, you'd take a break for lunch and a quick nap before heading back to class later in the afternoon. And don't even think about doodling to distract yourself or dozing off—ancient Egyptian teachers were super strict and would beat misbehaving students. Now that's harsh!

A SCHOOL FIT FOR A PRINCE

Royal kids may have had a cushy life (hello, palaces staffed with servants and endless all-you-can-eat buffets!), but they weren't off the hook when it came to education. The sons of pharaohs, plus members of the royal family, nobles, and high officials, went to an exclusive school. There they'd be taught by the best of the best and receive top-notch training on how to become future leaders of Egypt. You'd never hear one of these elite kids brag about their status, though. One of the key principles of ancient Egyptian education was the art of staying humble.

A HIGHER DEGREE

School didn't last as long as it does today. By their mid-teens, Egyptians were considered adults—and it was time to get a job or start a family. There were some exceptions, though. Later on in the Egyptian civilization, after Alexander the Great conquered the country, a university was opened by Greek scholars. The coolest thing about attending college? It was totally free—and there was no time limit to finishing a degree, so some students stayed in school for 12 to 14 years!

WHAT ABOUT THE GIRLS?

There's not much to show that girls went to school, although some records suggest that the daughters of nobles and royals did learn to read and write (a few may have even become scribes!). But the majority of girls were homeschooled by their mothers, who would teach them life skills like cooking, sewing, math, and music so they could take care of their own family one day.

DREAM ON!

Students didn't just learn the basic subjects in school—some of them were dedicated to dreamier matter, literally! Priests, in particular, could become "masters of the secret things," or dream interpreters, by studying at the House of Life, an education center found in each ancient Egyptian town. Because Egyptians believed that the gods spoke to them in their sleep, it was important to have a professional explain any warnings or advice delivered by the deities in dreams. So, not only did future priests learn things like taking care of temples and making mummies in school, they also studied the symbolism of different dreams.

My dream job

DIG IT!

Artifacts from an ancient Egyptian school show that teachers wrote quotes on the walls for students to copy.

Life at Home
Inside the DAILY LIVES of Ancient Egyptians

FAMILY FIRST

Families were everything in ancient Egypt. In the average household, grandparents, parents, kids, and pets all lived under one roof as one big, happy unit that did mostly everything together. Typically, the head of the household was a man who took charge of finances and discipline. His wife covered all the household's daily duties, like cooking and sewing.

WELCOME HOME

The typical Egyptian family lived in a two- or three-story building made out of mud bricks. These diminutive dwellings were about the size of a large bedroom, but the inventive Egyptians made these tiny spaces work!

HOME, SWEET (FANCY) HOME

While the royal family lived on palatial estates, the upper class didn't do too shabbily, either. Their homes were much larger than the commoners' dwellings—some having as many as 30 rooms!—with fancier features like toilets, tile floors, wood and leather furniture, and outdoor pools stocked with fish and flowers. How nice!

DIG IT!

Bricks used to build homes were made from straw mixed with mud from the Nile River and dried in the hot sun.

UP ON THE ROOF The house's roof was flat and offered some bonus outdoor living space. Families sometimes slept up there, too!

LOOK OUT Windows were placed higher in the house to keep the sand out. They usually had barriers to keep wild animals away.

ALL WHITE The outside of the house was usually painted white to keep it cooler in the sweltering desert heat. Wealthier Egyptians built their homes with a layer of white limestone on the outside, but paint was a cheaper solution.

BARE NECESSITIES Egyptian families didn't use much furniture. Beds were usually straw mats on the floor, and Egyptians would rest their heads on stone or wooden headrests. Sweet dreams?

HIT THE DIRT Who needs hardwood flooring when you've got dirt? These homes usually had dirt floors covered with mats or rugs to sit on.

Dress Like an Egyptian
Ancient Egyptian FASHION

MANY YOUNG **KIDS** **DIDN'T** **WEAR** **CLOTHES** UNTIL THEY WERE **TEENAGERS.**

PHARAOH FASHION

Ancient Egyptian fashion was all about beating the heat. So they stuck to lightweight materials that could keep them cool, fashioning them into long dresses for the ladies or kilts fastened around the waist for the men.

STATUS SYMBOLS

The Egyptians didn't go any- where without their acces- sories! Jewelry was just as much a part of their everyday outfits as linen dresses and kilts. Men and women often wore large earrings, rings, bracelets, and necklaces made of gold and copper and accented with colorful beads. So why so much bling?

Besides being a way to show off their sta- tus, Egyptians believed some jewelry had magical pow- ers—especially amulets, the pendants crafted into the shape of gods or hieroglyphs. These were worn or car- ried to protect people from harm—and were also bur- ied with mummies for good luck in the afterlife.

HAIR FOR SALE

How'd they make those wigs? Some women would chop their locks and sell them to wigmakers. People with deeper pockets would have a wig made of 100 per- cent human hair, while others would have to settle for sheep's wool. *Baa*-eautiful!

DIG IT!
Wigs were styled with beeswax and kept shiny with a combo of oil and boiled animal's blood.

WASH OUT

Ancient Egyptians had to do simple chores just like we do, including the laundry. While the royal family had hired help to do their dirty work (royal chief washer and royal chief bleacher were actual jobs!), average folks would sim- ply haul their clothes down to the Nile to soak in the river water before scrubbing them with a special cleaner called natron. Then they'd dry them out in the sun before folding and putting the clothes away. Ancient Egyptians ... they're just like us!

HEAD GAMES Egyptians rarely left home without a headpiece. These toppers told a person's position in society (the fancier the headdress, the higher up you were). Pharaohs would always wear a crown or a royal head cloth to cover up their locks.

GET WIGGY WITH IT Wigs were in back then, often seen on noble men and women—who would accessorize their 'do with a glitzy headband or a fragrant lotus flower.

ALL THAT GLITTERS Pharaohs and non-royals alike wore a sparkling collar called a *wesekh*, often made with golden beads and precious jewels.

FACE TIME A clean-shaven face kept men cool in the dry desert heat, but pharaohs would often wear fake beards as a sign of wisdom and to mimic the look of the god Osiris.

LEATHER BOUND While the average person wore sandals made from papyrus, thick leather shoes were a status symbol among the rich. Funny enough, there are stories of Egyptians wearing their sandals at home but going barefoot outside.

ROYAL LINEN Wealthy people wore dresses or kilts made of supersoft linen cloth. The cloth came from flax stems, which were dried up and rolled to make threads, then woven on a loom to form cloth.

Egyptian Makeup
Ancient BEAUTY RITUALS

AN ANCIENT BURIAL MASK HIGHLIGHTS THE POPULARITY OF EYELINER.

DIG IT!
Egyptian women used burnt almonds to paint their eyebrows black.

MAGICAL MAKEUP

The Egyptians believed that wearing makeup gave them the protection of the gods Horus and Atum. The *Book of the Dead,* the famed manuscript that mapped the journey to the afterlife, mentions that one should "make up his eyes and anoint himself" before being judged by Osiris. Even the way the makeup was applied—in an almond-shape outline around the eyes—was a nod to the spirits, since it looked a lot like the shape of a falcon's eye. And because Horus was the falcon god who protected the kingdom, it made sense that they wanted to look just like him.

MORE THAN SKIN-DEEP

The iconic images of Cleopatra may have made thick eyeliner famous, but many Egyptians before her time were sporting similar make-up styles. Eyelids rimmed in black or green kohl—made from minerals plucked from the Sahara—was such a common look in ancient times that almost *everyone*, both men and women, from peasants to pharaohs, sported it daily. Even babies could be spotted crawling around wearing extravagant eye makeup.

So when did the look originate? Experts aren't so sure. But they do know that the makeup wasn't just meant to make people's eyes stand out. It was likely a way to protect the eyes from the sun's glare, as well as to keep their eyes healthy. Because the makeup was made from materials that could potentially block bacteria, it may have kept the Egyptians from picking up icky infections like pink eye.

LIP SERVICE

Red lips were all the rage in ancient Egypt. The bright rosy hue was super common on women, and they made it by grinding up a mineral called hematite. Later, when Cleopatra came along, the practice of crushing the shells of bugs like ants and beetles to get a bold hue became popular. Some cosmetic companies continue to use this type of pigment—also known as carmine—today!

PIECES OF THE PAST! COSMETIC CLUES

Researchers have been able to piece together the Egyptians' beauty routine based on the many items they left behind. Tools like tweezers, razors, combs, and mirrors made out of copper and bronze all indicate that self-care was super important in their lives. They also fashioned skinny sticks and wands to apply their makeup as well as tubes and pots to store it. How fashion-forward!

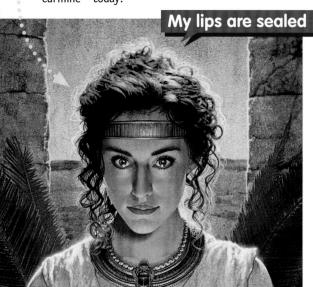

My lips are sealed

SOME ANCIENT **EGYPTIANS MADE MOISTURIZER** OUT OF **WHIPPED OSTRICH EGGS, OLIVE OIL, MILK,** AND SEA SALT.

Eat Up!
What the Ancient Egyptians ATE

How did the Egyptians fill their bellies? With a lot of the same foods we munch on in modern times. Because of the Nile Valley's fertile soil and the Egyptians' excellent farming system, food was fairly plentiful during good flood years. While everyone ate pretty well back then, your status in society definitely determined just what you put on your plate.

IF YOU WERE AN ORDINARY EGYPTIAN

SLICE OF LIFE

Bread was a staple for everyone, especially average Egyptians, who'd bake their own loaves in a clay oven or over a charcoal fire.

GO GREEN!

The Egyptians had no problem eating their veggies! Their favorites? Cucumbers, lettuce, and radishes—which they'd often eat boiled.

SMALL BITES

Grapes and nabk fruit (which tasted like apples) were easy-to-obtain sweet treats.

IF YOU WERE A WEALTHY NOBLE

SPICE IT UP!

Spice was a fixture of any Egyptian feast. Since the world's major trading routes passed through the country, Egyptians had easy access to exotic eastern spices. They flavored their food with spices still used today, like cumin, fennel, thyme, and garlic. Yum!

MORE MEAT

Cuts of meat were pricey in ancient Egypt, so only the rich feasted on sheep, duck, ox, and even wild animals like antelope.

FRESH FRUIT

Fruits like melons and pomegranates (imported from other countries) were gobbled up ... seeds and all.

SUGAR, SUGAR

The Egyptians loved their sweets! Cakes made with fruits, nuts, and seeds and sweetened with dates, figs, and honey were staples at most meals.

OH, HONEY

Since the golden, sticky sweetener was used on nearly everything, Egyptians kept bees on their property to harvest their own honey.

SAY CHEESE

Dairy didn't keep well in the Egyptian heat, so they made their milk into cheese and yogurt.

SOME ANCIENT EGYPTIANS WOULD EAT **DRIED AND SALTED** (AND STINKY!) **FISH** THAT HAD **WASHED UP** ON THE SHORES OF **THE NILE.**

Good Sports!

KOOKY COMPETITIONS in Ancient Egypt

PLAY ON!

The Egyptians loved to watch a good game or competition! Artifacts dating back to 1190 B.C. show people packing grandstands to watch wrestling, boxing, and fencing. Ancient documents reveal that the winners of some competitions took home prizes of cows, cloaks, and animal skins. Who needs a gold medal?

LIKE A GIRL

In ancient Egypt, girls had game, too! Artwork shows school-age girls doing gymnastics, dancing, juggling, swimming, and boating. As for the boys? They stuck to team sports, like field hockey, or wrestling, rowing, and boxing.

EXTREME EGYPT

While the ancient Egyptians played sports similar to the ones we still play, they tended to take it up a notch. Take wrestling, for example. They'd go against each other in pairs of two, with one person carrying the other piggy-back (kids in Egypt liked to play catch this way, too). Tug-of-war was a thing, too, but not in the way we know it. Instead of a rope, young Egyptian boys would link hands and pull each other's arms apart. Now *that's* an extreme sport!

ONE **4,600-YEAR-OLD** TOMB PAINTING SHOWS ANCIENT EGYPTIANS **OIL WRESTLING.**

SO SPORTY

Egyptians and sports go *way* back. Several thousands of years, to be exact! Inscriptions on ancient monuments tell of a civilization for which sports were a big deal, much like they are in our world today. Athletic events were a part of the king's coronation, celebrations of military victories, religious ceremonies, and festivals, complete with rules, refs, and even uniforms. Some of the sports they played are a lot like the ones still popular today. Here are some sports that have stood the test of time!

A SPORT SIMILAR TO...

FIELD HOCKEY

GO-TO GEAR: A stick made out of a palm tree branch with a slight bend at the end; a ball made from crushed papyrus fibers, covered in leather.

RULES OF THE GAME: Two teams matched up on a patch of dry desert to try to navigate the ball into a goal.

WEIGHT LIFTING

GO-TO GEAR: A heavy sack filled with sand.

RULES OF THE GAME: Lift the sack with one hand and hoist it over your head as high as you can.

JUGGLING

GO-TO GEAR: Balls similar to those used in field hockey, sometimes dyed in different colors.

RULES OF THE GAME: Tomb paintings show Egyptians expertly tossing as many as six balls in the air.

BOWLING

GO-TO GEAR: Different-size balls, and a long room with a hollow square at the center.

RULES OF THE GAME: One person rolls a ball toward a hole in the middle of the room. Meanwhile, other people roll their own balls of different sizes toward the same hole, trying to knock their opponent's ball off course.

WHITE-WATER RAFTING

GO-TO GEAR: A small boat made out of papyrus.

RULES OF THE GAME: Two people in one boat try to navigate the choppy and swift-moving rapids of the Nile River, also known as the cataracts, while onlookers cheer them on from the banks.

ARCHERY

GO-TO GEAR: A bow, an arrow, and copper targets.

RULES OF THE GAME: A favorite sport of the royals, pharaohs would shoot arrows at a target while riding a chariot or a horse.

They've Got Game

FAVORITE ACTIVITIES of the Ancient Egyptians

A PAINTING OF QUEEN NEFERTARI PLAYING THE GAME OF SENET

The Egyptians loved to play around! In fact, they are considered the first civilization to play sports with balls, and they also came up with one of the world's oldest board games. Here's some more of their ancient activities.

SENET

THE GIST:
The rules aren't known, but experts think this board game was based on the struggle between good and evil—and the journey to the afterlife. Two players would throw sticks (in the same way we throw dice) to see how many squares they'd move on the board. Each square had a different picture on it. Land on a square with a happy picture, and you were good to go. Land on one that represented evil, and it was no afterlife for you!

WINNING FACT: *Senet* was so popular that some wall paintings reveal animals like lions and antelope playing the game.

DIG IT!
The Egyptians played a game just like tic-tac-toe more than 3,000 years ago.

MEHEN

THE GIST: Also known as the snake game, it featured a stone board representing a coiled serpent. While experts think the objective was to get your piece to the middle of the coil, no one knows for sure since no rules have ever been found.

WINNING FACT: The game pieces were shaped like dogs or lions, or stones smoothed into round balls and etched with a hieroglyph of a pharaoh's name.

TUT'S GAMES

King Tut may have been a gamer! A search of his tomb revealed four Senet boards, including one carefully crafted out of pricey ebony and ivory resting on four wooden legs carved to look like animals' legs. There was also a smaller travel set made of painted ivory, likely there to make sure Tut was set up to play Senet whenever—and wherever—he wanted once he reached the afterlife.

SEKER-HEMAT

THE GIST: Somewhat similar to baseball, one player—typically, a pharaoh—would use a stick to whack at a ball. Priests served as the fielders.

WINNING FACT: The ball actually represented the eye of a monstrous serpent. A smack of the ball symbolized crushing evil. Score!

KHUZZA LAWIZZA

THE GIST: Like an ancient version of leapfrog, two players sit on the floor facing each other, extend their arms out in front, and touch hands. A third player jumps over their outstretched arms without touching them.

WINNING FACT: The game, now known as goose steps, is still played in Egypt today.

Child's Play!
LIFE AS A KID in Ancient Egypt

KIDDING AROUND

Life wasn't *all* fun and games in ancient Egypt. Most people worked very hard to make a living for their families. But no matter what, adults tried to make a point of keeping things light for their little ones. After all, you were only a kid for so long: By their mid-teens, boys and girls were often expected to take on jobs, get married, and start a family of their own!

PROTECTIVE PARENTS

Most parents in ancient Egypt were super protective. And rightfully so. After all, kids faced a bit more danger than they do today: There were more sicknesses and diseases back then, plus creatures like scorpions and snakes were known to attack little ones left unattended. So from the start, kids were constantly cared for and protected by their parents. To keep kids out of harm's way, a mom—or an older sibling—would typically carry a baby or toddler around in a soft sling at all times. Parents would also chant spells and wear special amulets to keep their kids safe. And you thought *your* parents were overprotective!

HAVING A BALL

Scary stuff aside, kids had plenty of time to play, too! We already know about many of the sports and games they got into back then. Children were often spotted outside playing, since their homes were on the small side. They also had a trove of toys to keep them entertained. Archaeological digs and wall paintings reveal that kids were pretty crafty: They'd make their own tops, rattles, and balls out of stuff found around their house, like pebbles, pieces of wood, sand, and plants. There's even evidence that kids would make dolls out of wooden pegs wrapped in cloth. Now that's creative!

PIECES OF THE PAST!
TOMB DOLLS

Sure, it made sense that the ancient Egyptians buried younger folks with toys to play with in the afterlife. But studies of tombs have revealed that some grown women were laid to rest alongside paddle dolls. So what's the deal? Experts think that the dolls weren't toys, but rather symbols of fertility and rebirth. The Egyptians likely believed that the dolls—which were often decorated with images of the goddess Taweret, who protected pregnant women—were good luck charms that would give a woman a chance to have babies in the afterlife.

TOP TOYS

Ancient Egyptian kids played with toys similar to what we have today!

ROLL ON

Experts think this painted wooden horse with wheels is likely more than 2,000 years old!

MAKE YOUR MOVE

This game piece, shaped like a lion, was found in the Osiris temple.

SHAKE IT UP

Dice games were so popular in ancient Egypt that sets of dice have been found in some tombs.

HIP HIPPO HOORAY

Not only did the Egyptians worship animals like the hippo, they also made games out of them!

NO BONES ABOUT IT

This figurine—likely used as a mini toy or a game piece—was carved out of bone.

Awesome Egyptian Inventions

The Things We Can THANK THE ANCIENT EGYPTIANS FOR

DIG IT!

Egyptian farmers created an early version of a plow more than 6,000 years ago!

EARLY INNOVATORS

The Egyptians were inventive people! Not only did they come up with innovative ideas like the pyramids, mummification, and the written language, they also introduced more everyday items. From calendars to clocks and toothpaste to tools, many Egyptian inventions set the stage for stuff that we still use today.

BY THE NUMBERS

In ancient Egypt, math helped people understand the world around them. Take, for example, the building of the pyramids. Without a standard way to measure things like the stones used to form the massive structures, they wouldn't be able to design them with such careful precision. So they came up with a unit of length called the cubit, which was equal to the length between a person's elbow and the tip of the middle finger (about 18 inches [46 cm]). The Egyptians used cubits to measure everything from tombs to coffins—and the unit caught on among other ancient civilizations. In fact, in the Bible, Noah's ark was said to measure 30 cubits high and 50 cubits wide.

SAVE THE DATE

Can you imagine life without a calendar? Life would be pretty confusing without knowing the days of the week or the seasons. Way back in the day, the Egyptians had no way of knowing when the Nile River would flood, so they came up with a way to chart it. First, they identified three three-month-long seasons: The flooding season, the planting season, and the harvest season. They also used math and astronomy to invent a sundial, which divided the day into morning and afternoon, and they eventually defined one day as a 24-hour block. All together, those three seasons added up to create the first 365-day annual calendar.

PURE GLASS

With the Sahara covering a lot of Egypt, it's no wonder Egyptians used sand to make stuff, namely glass. They perfected a way to melt sand into glass in a superhot furnace, then blow, or form, the glass. The result? Glass sculptures, beads, amulets, and other types of jewelry, plus jars and drinking glasses.

A **FAKE TOE** FOUND ON AN EGYPTIAN MUMMY MAY BE THE **FIRST EVER PROSTHETIC BODY PART.**

Good Hygiene
Thank the Egyptians for THESE TOILETRIES

DIG IT!
Egyptian dentists also used honey, ground wheat, and crushed fruit to fill cavities.

BREATH OF FRESH AIR

Self-care and hygiene were super important to Egyptians. Starting with their breath. The food they ate—made with lots of gritty grains and even sand baked into their bread—wore down the protective outer layer of their teeth, causing cavities that led to smelly decay and infections. Not to mention they ate onion and garlic on the regular. So they came up with a way to do away with dragon breath. Ancient artifacts reveal that the Egyptians created both toothpaste and mints to keep their mouths minty fresh.

CHEW ON THIS

Except it wasn't really that minty. The toothpaste—made of ox hooves, burned eggshells, volcanic rock, and an oil called myrrh—was more of a foul-tasting cleaner than a breath freshener. And as for the breath mints, they were pellets formed from boiling honey, cinnamon, myrrh, and sometimes, tree bark. These may not have offered the superfresh feeling that we know of today, but the pellets paved the way for modern mints.

PIECES OF THE PAST!
BRUSH ON

So we know that ancient Egyptians created toothpaste. But how, exactly, did they get the stuff on their teeth? Experts say they created their own toothbrushes, too! Or shall we say tooth*sticks.* Crafted from twigs with frayed ends to brush away bits of food, these ancient toiletries, dating back to 3500 B.C., were discovered in Egyptian tombs next to their owners. This means that even way back when, the Egyptians knew the importance of traveling with a toothbrush—even when you're heading to the afterlife.

EAU DE PORRIDGE?

And when it came to their overall odor? The Egyptians invented the perfumed bath, scented with aromatic oils, and also used incense and porridge on their bodies to try to mask any unpleasant smells. They also figured out a way to mask funky smells by creating scented pellets, which they'd store in their armpits. It is said that some women even placed cones of sweet-smelling wax on their heads that would melt throughout the day. Was it the cleanest method? Nope. But at least they smelled good.

ALL THE ACCESSORIES

Egyptians are also credited for coming up with combs, hairpins, razors, and handheld mirrors—all signs that point to the high value they placed on looking (and smelling) good.

THE ANCIENT EGYPTIANS WASHED UP WITH A SOAP PASTE MADE OUT OF CLAY AND OLIVE OIL.

The Doctor Is In!
Ancient Egyptian MEDICINE

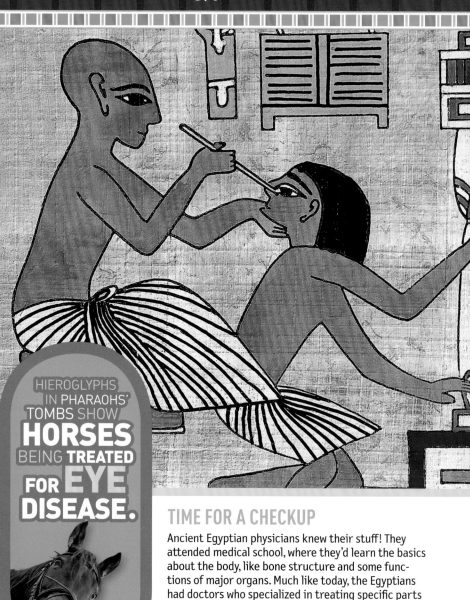

HIEROGLYPHS IN PHARAOHS' TOMBS SHOW **HORSES** BEING **TREATED** FOR **EYE DISEASE.**

TIME FOR A CHECKUP

Ancient Egyptian physicians knew their stuff! They attended medical school, where they'd learn the basics about the body, like bone structure and some functions of major organs. Much like today, the Egyptians had doctors who specialized in treating specific parts of the body, giving them kooky titles like "Royal Keeper of the Pharaoh's Left Eye." This expertise gave them a reputation of being the best doctors in the world. So it's no surprise that they were sought after by kings and queens from faraway lands.

JUST WHAT THE DOCTOR ORDERED

Have a headache? Rub some boiled catfish on your noggin. Feeling a cough coming on? Cook a mouse whole, grind it up, and then down it with a glass of milk. These cures may make you sick just thinking about them, but they were standard practice for ancient Egyptian doctors, who had some downright bizarre ideas about healing people. Back then, a lot of medicine was about using easy-to-access items—like herbs, plants, food, and yes, even animal parts—to keep the doctor away. So much for an apple a day.

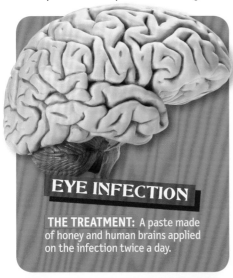

WHOOPING COUGH

THE TREATMENT: A "smoothie" made out of whole roasted mouse, ground up and mixed with milk!

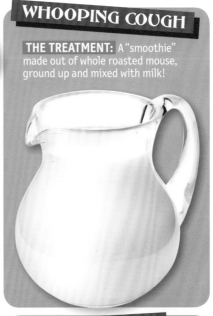

EYE INFECTION

THE TREATMENT: A paste made of honey and human brains applied on the infection twice a day.

FRACTURED SKULL

THE TREATMENT: First, any broken bits of bone in the skull were patched up with a putty made up of ground-up ostrich eggshell and oil. Then, the head would be wrapped in bandages for three days to let the putty dry.

TOOTHACHE

THE TREATMENT: Doctors would spread a paste of mashed mouse onto the sore tooth.

SKIN INFECTION

THE TREATMENT: The wound would be bandaged with moldy bread or a cut of fresh meat.

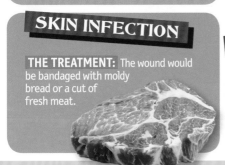

TAPEWORM

THE TREATMENT: A drink made up of equal parts lead, petroleum, bread, and sweet beer.

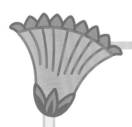

THE TRUTH BEHIND THE ICK

There was somewhat of a method behind the madness of ancient Egyptian medicine. Thousands of years after Egyptians plastered moldy bread on wounds, scientists discovered that certain fungi, like mold, are known to block the growth of disease-causing bacteria (which is where we got some antibiotics, like penicillin). And prescriptions like powdered liver offered a vitamin A boost, vital for vision.

BLAME THE GODS!

Ancient Egyptian medicine had plenty of influence from the spiritual side of things. In fact, doctors often chanted spells to ward off illnesses, since they thought some sicknesses were directly caused by the gods— or even that an evil spirit had entered the body. It was super common for people to wear magical charms known as amulets, which were believed to protect them and their health.

So what happened if you got hurt or fell sick? Likely, you'd see a healer, who would use a mix of magic and science to treat you. As outlined in the Ebers Papyrus—an ancient scroll that details some 700 remedies and spells—the Egyptians had a ritual to handle just about any health issue. Did the magical spells really work? Probably not. Experts think that the chants probably calmed the patients, but didn't do much to actually cure them.

UNDER THE KNIFE

Ancient Egyptian doctors didn't just slather animal poop on wounds, say a spell, and call it a day. Some of them performed basic surgeries on patients. Ancient medical tools like knives, pincers, forceps, spoons, and saws indicate that physicians did do operations, most likely to set broken bones, pull teeth, or treat issues close to the skin (doctors were also skilled in stitching up wounds). As for more invasive operations? The Egyptians didn't have a way to put their patients to sleep, numb their pain, or treat infections (because, let's face it: moldy bread doesn't always do the trick). So, most surgeries were kept close to the surface.

The Egyptians may have invented toothpaste, but that didn't keep them from getting cavities! And plenty of them. In 2012, researchers performing a high-res scan on a 2,100-year-old mummy discovered that the man had a mouthful of cavities, which likely caused an infection that wound up killing him. But not before he saw a dentist— also known as "the one who is concerned with teeth." Researchers also found a piece of linen stuffed into one of the largest cavities, which they believe was meant to serve as a barrier to block food from getting trapped in the gap. The linen was likely dipped in fig juice or cedar oil to help ease the pain. That may have worked as a temporary fix, but researchers think the man died soon after of his infection. Just another reason to get those regular six-month checkups!

ANCIENT EGYPTIAN ART SHOWING DIFFERENT MEDICAL INSTRUMENTS

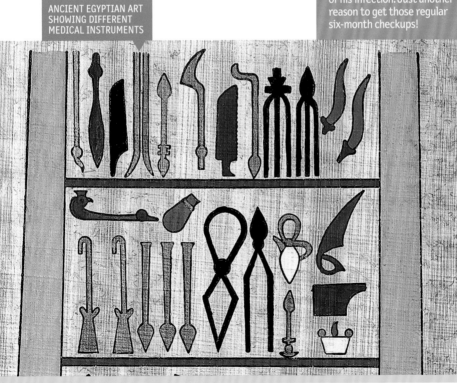

Cool Tools
Four Handy Egyptian INVENTIONS

The Egyptians didn't have machines to do their dirty work, so they had to build everything by hand. Which was why it was key to come up with tools to help them complete a task. Here are four they invented.

ADZE

HOW IT WORKED: A metal blade attached by leather straps to a wooden shaft, this tool was used for smoothing out surfaces like boat hulls, or to carve large items like coffins.

PLOW

HOW IT WORKED: Originally, the plow was a lightweight tool that was pulled by up to four men—a tough task in the blazing Egyptian sun. Eventually, they switched over to ox-pulled plows, which made farming that much more effective—and so much easier on the farmer.

SICKLE

HOW IT WORKED: A curved blade made from wood, glazed and filed to create a sharp edge. It was used to cut grains like wheat and barley in the fields.

OTHER INVENTIONS!

The list goes on and on! Three more famous items we owe to the Egyptians ...

- **DOOR LOCKS:** Featuring a bolt and key, the locks were used to protect homes.
- **SMALL AREA RUGS:** Made with papyrus plants, they were used to cover the floors in Egyptian homes much like they still are today.
- **HOME DECOR:** Small statues—typically of Egypt's favorite gods and animals—were all the rage, making Egypt the first known culture to add religious decor and shrines in their homes.

SCISSORS

HOW IT WORKED: Made from two blades connected by a metal strip. Just squeeze the handles, and the blades would cross over and cut whatever was in between them.

What's it like to study ancient Egypt for a living?

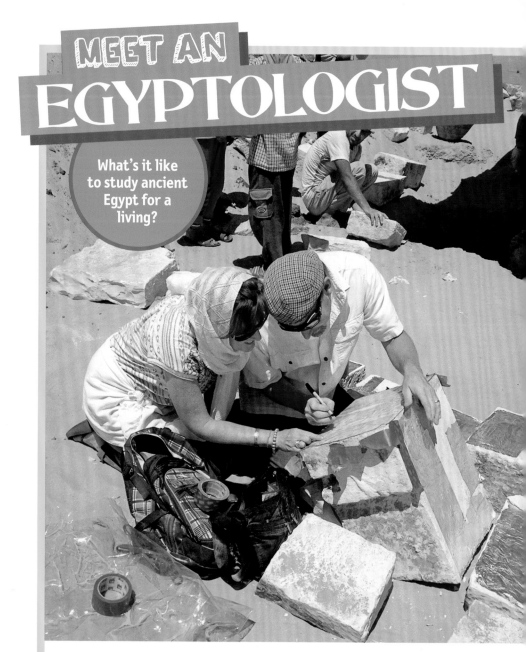

Imagine getting paid to mull over mummies, study hieroglyphs, or dig up artifacts. If you're an Egyptologist, that's just how you earn your paycheck! Anyone who focuses on the specific study of ancient Egypt is known as an Egyptologist. And by dedicating their time to the study of ancient Egypt, these experts have been able to shed light on this culture's mysterious past and answer questions that have been alluding us for centuries. Want to know more about this cool career? Read on for more from an actual Egyptologist.

JENNIFER HOUSER WEGNER

WHO: Dr. Jennifer Houser Wegner
WHAT: Associate curator in the Egyptian Section at the University of Pennsylvania Museum of Archaeology and Anthropology
WHERE: Philadelphia, Pennsylvania, U.S.A.

What does a typical day on the job look like for you?

Our museum has 50,000 objects from Egypt, many of which came from excavations our museum carried out over the last 100 years. I work with objects, carry out research and writing, and plan exhibits.

Do you ever travel to Egypt?

I sometimes travel to Egypt, where I work on a project at the site of Abydos. There we are working in an area with materials that date to about 2000–1500 B.C. The best part about being an Egyptologist is going to Egypt and working at the site!

What inspired you to become an Egyptologist?

In sixth grade, I had a fantastic teacher who really brought the past to life and got me into ancient Egypt. From that point on, I knew that I wanted to study Egyptology and have a career in the field.

Do you specialize in one area of ancient Egypt in particular?

My specialization is ancient Egyptian language. Specifically, the language known as Demotic. It's a cursive script that was used late in Egypt's history, and is one of the three scripts on the Rosetta Stone, along with hieroglyphs and Greek.

What's one of the coolest things that's happened to you on the job?

It was incredible visiting the site of Abydos. The team discovered the tomb of a previously unknown pharaoh by the name of Senebkay, who lived around 1650 B.C. His skeleton was still in the tomb. That was exciting!

What do you find most fascinating about the ancient Egyptian civilization?

Even though the ancient Egyptians lived thousands of years ago and it seems like their lives were very different from ours, they were human beings just like us. They had hopes and dreams, and they solved problems. Examining their lives and the materials they left behind might help us understand the world better.

SO YOU WANT TO BE AN EGYPTOLOGIST?

Want to dig into Egyptology? Reading this book is a great first step! Dr. Houser Wegner also suggests checking out local museums with Egyptian collections, as well as camps or programs at your library or a nearby university that focus on ancient Egypt. And stay curious about all kinds of history! As Dr. Houser Wegner says, "The past can tell us about the present."

MAJOR DISCOVERIES

Experts have been making fascinating finds from ancient Egypt for centuries. And they continue to unearth amazing things today. Here's a timeline detailing some of the most dynamic discoveries from ancient Egypt.

THE ROSETTA STONE

1799

During Napoleon's invasion of Egypt, a soldier discovers a black slab with ancient writing etched into it near the town of Rosetta, near Alexandria. Containing fragments of passages written in three different scripts— Greek, Egyptian hieroglyphs, and Egyptian Demotic—the Rosetta Stone ultimately allows experts to under- stand and translate hieroglyphs.

| 1790 | 1800 | 1890 | 1900 | 1910 |

NEFERTITI'S PAINTED BUST

1912

German archaeologist Ludwig Borchardt uncovers the 3,300-year-old limestone bust of the ancient queen within the remains of a sculptor's workshop. The bust becomes a long-lasting symbol of beauty and girl power.

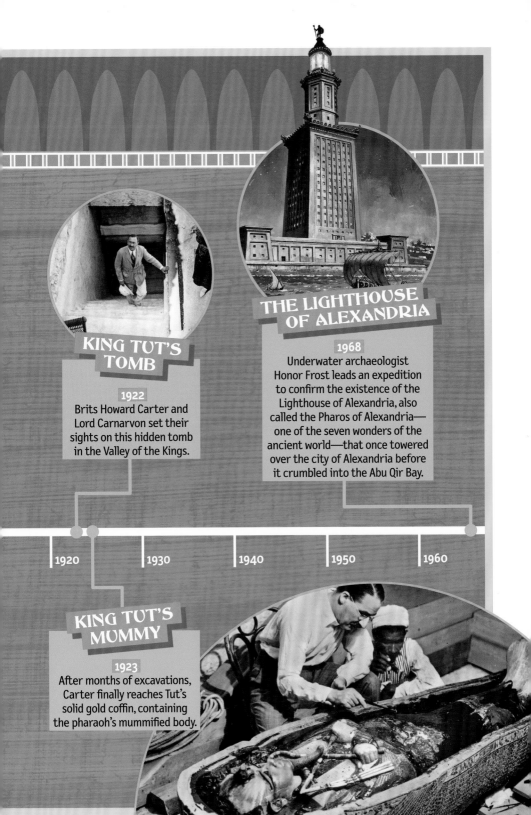

THE LIGHTHOUSE OF ALEXANDRIA

1968

Underwater archaeologist Honor Frost leads an expedition to confirm the existence of the Lighthouse of Alexandria, also called the Pharos of Alexandria—one of the seven wonders of the ancient world—that once towered over the city of Alexandria before it crumbled into the Abu Qir Bay.

KING TUT'S TOMB

1922

Brits Howard Carter and Lord Carnarvon set their sights on this hidden tomb in the Valley of the Kings.

1920   1930   1940   1950   1960

KING TUT'S MUMMY

1923

After months of excavations, Carter finally reaches Tut's solid gold coffin, containing the pharaoh's mummified body.

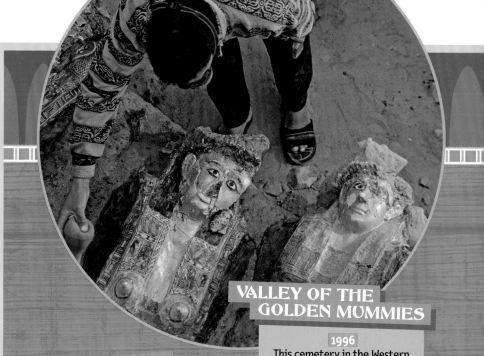

VALLEY OF THE GOLDEN MUMMIES

1996

This cemetery in the Western Desert, some 236 miles (380 km) from the pyramids, is found accidentally when a donkey steps into a hole and its owner spots a glint of gold underground. Soon, thousands of mummies are uncovered, some with golden masks, telling us more about the time when Greece and Rome ruled Egypt.

TOMB KV5

1987

American Egyptologist Dr. Kent Weeks uncovers the entrance of the largest tomb known to date. Located in the Valley of the Kings, the tomb belongs to several sons of Ramses II, who ruled ancient Egypt for 67 years.

1970   1980   1990   2000

CLEOPATRA'S PALACE

1998

The palace—in pieces after being toppled by an earthquake and swallowed by the ocean— is located by a team of divers led by French underwater archaeologist Franck Goddio some 25 feet (7.6 m) beneath the surface of the Mediterranean Sea. The search eventually recovers at least 20,000 ancient objects.

WORKERS' VILLAGE AT GIZA

2002

American archaeologist Mark Lehner unearths a town believed to have been home to as many as 20,000 people some 4,500 years ago. Located near the Sphinx, the village reveals details about the people who built the pyramids and their daily lives.

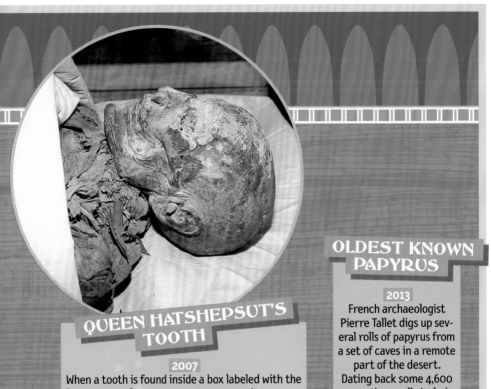

QUEEN HATSHEPSUT'S TOOTH

2007

When a tooth is found inside a box labeled with the famous queen's name, experts compare it to a scan of the mouth of a mysterious mummy found years before. Turns out the tooth fits, and the mummy is identified as Hatshepsut.

OLDEST KNOWN PAPYRUS

2013

French archaeologist Pierre Tallet digs up several rolls of papyrus from a set of caves in a remote part of the desert. Dating back some 4,600 years, the scrolls include a first-person account of how the Great Pyramid at Giza was built.

2010

2020

HETPET'S TOMB

2018

A 4,400-year-old tomb discovered near the Giza pyramids belongs to Hetpet, a female priest from the 5th dynasty. Decorated with paintings showing her hunting, fishing, and dancing, the tomb offers a unique look at the life of one of the most powerful women of her time.

7 COOL FACTS ABOUT EGYPT

There's so much more to Egypt than the Nile River and ruins. Today, the country is home to more than 88 million people and counting, has a bustling capital city, and is considered the modern hub of Africa. Want to learn more? Here are seven things you might not know about Egypt.

① CROCODILES (STILL) LIVE HERE.

The reptiles have been roaming the banks of the Nile for thousands of years. Today, they mostly live in Lake Nasser, a human-made lake in southern Egypt.

② WHALES ONCE WALKED HERE.

Some 40 million years ago, whales with hind legs strolled along the banks of the Nile. Now, all that's left of these ancient animals are massive fossils found in Wadi Al-Hitan (Valley of the Whales), a protected area less than 100 miles (161 km) from Cairo. Over time, the whales evolved and lost their legs, becoming the sea-based swimmers we know and love today.

③ IT'S HOME TO THE WORLD'S LARGEST PAIR OF UNDERPANTS.

Yep, you read that right. A Cairo-based cotton company crafted a behemoth pair of boxer briefs with a waist wider than two city buses.

④ YOU CAN SURF THE SAND.

With so much of the country covered by desert, it's no surprise that sand-boarding is a popular sport. Active people flock to the Great Sand Sea near Siwa to cruise down steep dunes that soar to heights of 450 feet (137 m).

⑤ CAMEL RACING RULES.

An annual camel festival in Ismailia, Egypt, attracts enthusiasts from all over the world to watch camels go hoof to hoof. The races—a tradition of the nomadic Bedouin tribe—typically involve lightweight jockeys who are sometimes as young as eight years old!

⑥ IT HAS A MAJOR MUSEUM.

Old meets new at the supermodern Grand Egyptian Museum in Cairo. The $1 billion museum—the world's largest museum devoted to a single civiliza-tion—is home to some of the most famous finds from ancient times, including King Tut's sandals and the giant statue of Ramses II.

⑦ IT HAS A PHENOMENAL FOOD COURT.

The world's largest, in fact. The Oasis in Cairo has 25 restaurants, can seat 4,223 people, and has a parking lot big enough to fit 1,000 cars.

MYTHS BUSTED

As much as we know about ancient Egypt, a lot of its history remains a mystery. This has led some people to come up with some assumptions and downright wacky ideas to answer certain questions about the time period. Through tons of research, experts have debunked most of these myths—but they're still fun to think about!

CANNONBALL!

THE MYTH: Napoleon shot off the Great Sphinx's nose with a cannonball!

THE TRUTH REVEALED: Rumors circulated for years that the French military leader was to blame for the missing nose after getting trigger-happy during his 1798 invasion of Egypt. But evidence suggests that it was actually a religious fanatic named Muhammad Sa'im al-Dahr who intentionally lopped it off in the late 14th century. He was later executed for his crime.

THE SPARE ROOM!

THE MYTH: King Tut's tomb has secret chambers!

THE TRUTH REVEALED: For years, experts wondered if Tut's final resting spot contained hidden chambers. They even theorized that Queen Nefertiti's remains may be tucked away in the tomb. After analyzing numerous high-tech scans of the tomb, a team of researchers conclusively proved that there are no additional chambers or passages behind the walls. So the search for Nefertiti continues ...

ALIEN ARCHITECTS!

THE MYTH: Aliens built the pyramids!

THE TRUTH REVEALED: How else can you explain how millions of stones, weighing at least two tons (1.8 t) each, were put together to form pyramids without the help of cranes or other construction equipment? The feat may seem supernatural, but artifacts show that a team of several thousand earth-bound individuals built the pyramids and other massive structures the old-fashioned way: with a lot of hard work.

BURIED ALIVE!

THE MYTH: Pharaohs were buried with their servants!

THE TRUTH REVEALED: Legends told of pharaohs being so dependent on their trusty servants that they insisted on heading to the afterlife with them—even if the servant was, well, alive. There is some evidence that a few pharaohs from the 1st dynasty did demand that their dutiful servants be killed and then sealed in their tomb, but that practice didn't last long. Instead, a pharaoh's servants simply said their final goodbyes aboveground.

TUT MURDERED!

THE MYTH: King Tut was murdered!

THE TRUTH REVEALED: Could it be? Some tales told of the teen king being killed by his uncle, Ay, who went on to take the throne. While it's hard to imagine such a young king dying of natural causes, studies of his remains show that Tut succumbed to sickness, likely after being bitten by an infected mosquito.

SHIPWRECK!

THE MYTH: The *Titanic* was sunk by a mummy's curse!

THE TRUTH REVEALED: After the famous "unsinkable" ship went down in the Atlantic Ocean in 1912, rumors swirled of a cursed mummy of an Egyptian princess aboard the boat. The story goes that an American archaeologist paid for the mummy to be shipped to New York—and its presence caused the *Titanic* to sink. Turns out, no records show any mummy on board. And as we all know by now, the *Titanic*'s fate was sealed by an iceberg, not an unlucky mummy.

ANCIENT EGYPT'S HALL OF FAME

From awesome artifacts to major milestones, read all about record-breaking objects and moments from ancient Egypt that truly stood out—and have stood the test of time.

Peace out, dude

WHAT A ZOO Elephants and hippos and antelopes, oh my! The world's first zoo is believed to have been on a property in the ancient settlement of Hierakonpolis. The remains of 12 carefully buried animals—dating back to 3500 B.C.—were discovered near modern-day Luxor in 2009.

PEACE OUT When Ramses II and the king of the Hittites, Hattusilis II, agreed to end the years of warring between them in 1271 B.C., it marked the world's earliest known surviving peace treaty.

STEP IT UP The Step Pyramid at Saqqara gets the nod as the world's first major stone building. Before then, buildings were constructed from mud brick.

ALL THE KING'S HORSES

Oh *hay*, Ramses II! The famous pharaoh was an equine enthusiast. In fact, his horse stables—dating back to his reign more than 3,000 years ago—are believed to be the world's oldest. Big enough to house 460 horses, his herd had plenty of space to roam around: The stables covered an area around the same size as four soccer fields!

POWERFUL TOWER

Originally soaring to a height of 481 feet (147 m), the pyramid of Khufu—the Great Pyramid—is the tallest of them all. Although it has since shrunk some 30 feet (9 m) due to erosion, the pyramid still casts a powerful presence in Giza.

ANCIENT LETTERS

All hieroglyphs are old, but some are super old. A 5,300-year-old clay seal imprinted with the symbols is the earliest known example of Egyptian hieroglyphs.

DOG DAYS

Can you teach an old dog new tricks? Sure, if it's a saluki, the world's oldest breed of dog. It was a popular pet in ancient Egypt, especially among pharaohs, who often mummified their pooches to join them in the afterlife.

SIGN HERE

Move over, John Hancock! The first ever autograph on paper is believed to have been inked by an ancient Egyptian scribe on papyrus around 2130 B.C.

ON THE ROAD

Those giant stones didn't move themselves! So, to make it easier for them to transport huge boulders from quarries to the pyramid sites, the Egyptians laid what may have been the world's first paved road some 4,600 years ago. The 7.5-mile (12-km) stretch of road was covered with slabs of sandstone and limestone and logs of petrified wood.

WHICH PHARAOH ARE YOU?

Picture this: You've been teleported back to Egypt during ancient times, and you're about to claim the title of pharaoh. So, what kind of king or queen will you be? Take this quiz to find out which pharaoh's ruling style fits your personality! It's OK if your result doesn't actually fit your true personality—this is just for fun!

1 It's a rainy day. How will you pass the time inside?

a. Making funny videos to send to your friends
b. Reading
c. Making a collage out of old magazines
d. Rearranging your room

2 Which competition would you most likely win?

a. Lego building
b. Acting
c. Graphic design
d. Persuasive writing

3 Pick the best word to describe you.

a. Funny
b. Passionate
c. Unique
d. Opinionated

4 What's your favorite class?

a. Art
b. Foreign language
c. Coding
d. Social studies

5 What's your spirit animal?

a. Dog
b. Fox
c. Cheetah
d. Chameleon

6 Where would you go for your dream vacation?

a. Disney World ... it's the Happiest Place on Earth!
b. Europe ... to explore medieval castles and pick up a new language.
c. Antarctica ... it would be cool to go somewhere super remote.
d. The Caribbean ... you love to have fun in the sun.

MOSTLY A'S

Your Pharaoh Match: Khufu. Whether it's starring in your school play or hamming it up for the camera, you are made to be in the spotlight. And just like Khufu built the Great Pyramid at Giza to leave a lasting legacy, you are destined to create big things. Keep putting yourself out there, and people will remember your name!

MOSTLY B'S

Your Pharaoh Match: Cleopatra. Smart, savvy, and a little bit sneaky, you use your brains and your witty personality to get what you want. Like Cleopatra, you are determined to go after big goals. You may not be out to take over other kingdoms, but your curiosity and thirst for knowledge will help you conquer your own dreams.

MOSTLY C'S

Your Pharaoh Match: Hatshepsut. Passionate, intelligent, and unique, you stand out among your peers. Whether it's your quirky sense of style or outside-the-box ideas, you are a true individual. Like Hatshepsut, the famous female pharaoh, you have a way of distinguishing yourself, in a good way. Your friends and family look up to you for your boundary-breaking ways.

MOSTLY D'S

Your Pharaoh Match: Akhenaten. To you, change is good! Your mom is serving spaghetti for dinner again? You take the reins and offer to whip up the meals for the rest of the week. Just like Akhenaten, the pharaoh famous for shaking things up by switching Egypt's religion, you're all about change when you think it's needed. And you have a way of influencing others to go your way.

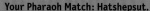

THROW AN ANCIENT EGYPT PARTY

Mad about mummies? Totally tuned into tombs? Whether you want to throw an ancient Egypt–themed extravaganza or a spooky soirée for your next Halloween bash, here's your go-to guide for a party that everyone will, uh, dig.

Eat This! Serve up these SPOOKY SNACKS.

MUMMY PRETZEL STICKS

INGREDIENTS: 1 bag of pretzel rods; 1 12-ounce (350 g) bag of candy melts in light cocoa; 1 12-ounce (350 g) bag of candy melts in white; and candy eyeballs (optional).

THE HOW-TO:

1. Line a baking sheet with wax paper.

2. Get a parent to help you melt the white candy melts according to the directions on the package.

3. Dip the top half of a pretzel rod in the white chocolate and lay it on the wax paper. Repeat until you've dipped your desired number of pretzels.

4. Dip a spoon in the melted candy melts, then carefully drizzle the liquid in zigzag lines across the part of the pretzel you've already dipped.

5. Add "eyes" to the mummies using candy eyeballs or use a dot of black icing or melted dark chocolate.

MUMMY MINI PIZZAS

INGREDIENTS: English muffins; jarred pizza sauce; sliced black olives; and mozzarella string cheese, pulled apart into thin pieces.

THE HOW-TO:

1. Have a parent help you split the English muffins.

2. Spread a tablespoon of pizza sauce onto each muffin half.

3. Crisscross the pieces of cheese on top of the sauce to create a mummy look.

4. Add two olive slices for eyes.

5. Place the mini pizzas on a cookie sheet.

6. Have a parent help you place the cookie sheet in the oven. Bake at 350°F (177°C) until the cheese bubbles, about 10 minutes.

Play This!

Turn up THE MUSIC— AND THE FUN—with this party game.

MUMMY MARCH

SUPPLIES: 1 chair for each guest; a *killer* party playlist.

THE HOW-TO:

I. Start the music. Have your guests walk around the chairs when the music starts.

2. As everyone marches around, have each guest offer their best mummy impression!

3. When the music stops, every-one must find a chair to sit on.

4. The guest who doesn't get a chair is eliminated.

5. Remove one more chair and play again.

6. Continue playing rounds until there's just one player left. The last mummy sitting wins!

Your PARTY PLAYLIST!

Set the tone by playing these retro tunes on repeat.

- "Walk Like an Egyptian," by the Bangles
- "Monster Mash," by Bobby Pickett
- "Africa," by Toto
- "I Put a Spell on You," by Nina Simone
- "Superstition," by Stevie Wonder
- "Somebody's Watching Me," by Rockwell
- "Rolling on the River," by Tina Turner
- "Time Warp," by Little Nell, Patricia Quinn, and Richard O'Brien

Give Your Guests This!

Your guests will be giddy to take home these WRAPPED UP party favors!

SUPPLIES: 1 inexpensive reusable water bottle for each guest (look for them in the dollar bin), 1 old white t-shirt, medium-size googly eyes, and glue.

THE HOW-TO:

I. Cut up each old t-shirt into thin strips (each strip should measure about 6 inches by 0.5 inches [15.3 by 1.3 cm]).

2. Wrap the strips around each bottle to make it look like a mummy. Secure with glue.

3. Glue two googly eyes onto the front of the bottle.

4. Fill with candy, snacks, or stickers and hand out to your guests! (When the party's over? They can remove the wrap and recycle the googly eyes and keep using the bottle.)

Make This!

HAVE YOUR GUESTS GET CRAFTY, and then send them home in style.

OH-SO-FAB PHARAOH COLLAR

SUPPLIES: White paper plates, paint and paint brushes (or markers), and scissors. Gems and anything shiny are all optional.

THE HOW-TO:

I. Cut a V-shape out of the top of the plate. Then cut along the plate's inside circle, so that you're left with a ring-shaped collar.

2. Paint the collar in bright colors and pat-terns. Add gems or glitter, if you wish.

3. Let the collar dry for an hour, and then wear it with pride!

CIVILIZATION:
The culture of a particular society that has reached an advanced level.

CUBIT:
A unit of measure used by ancient Egyptians. It was equal to the length between a person's elbow and the tip of the middle finger.

DEITY:
A god or goddess.

EGYPTOLOGIST:
Anyone who focuses on the specific study of ancient Egypt.

HIEROGLYPHS:
A complex system of symbols used as a way of storytelling and record-keeping among the ancient Egyptians. It is also the world's first known form of written communication.

KOHL:
A powder made from minerals and often used as eye makeup.

LIMESTONE:
A mineral formed mostly from the remains of tiny sea creatures.

MUMMY:
A dead body that has been preserved and wrapped in cloth.

NATRON:
A powdery salt used as a cleanser and in the mummification process.

NOMARCH:
A lawmaker who ruled over regions within Egypt, similar to today's mayors and governors.

OBELISK:
A tall, tapered tower often placed at the entrances of temples.

PAPYRUS:
A paper-like material used in ancient Egypt that was made from the crushed and pressed stems of the papyrus plant.

PHARAOH:
A king of ancient Egypt.

PYRAMID:
A large stone structure with sides that meet at a point. In ancient Egypt, pyramids were built to honor pharaohs, and were usually used as tombs.

REGISTERS:
Parallel lines used in ancient Egyptian art to create order and to separate scenes in a painting.

SCRIBE:
A person who recorded everything that went on in ancient Egypt—from laws and statistics to songs and religious texts.

SPHINX:
A mythological creature with a lion's body and a human's head; the huge stone statue of such a creature that is located in Egypt.

TEMPLE:
A building or place where a god or gods are worshipped.

TOMB:
A structure built to hold a dead body.

VIZIER:
The main adviser to the pharaoh.

INDEX

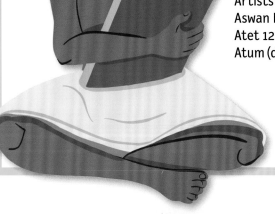

INDEX

INDEX

INDEX

INDEX

PHOTO CREDITS

Thank you to Ariane Szu-Tu and Kate Hale for your masterful editing.
To Dr. Jennifer Houser Wegner of the University of Pennsylvania
Museum of Archaeology and Anthropology for your expert consultation.
To my family for your endless and enthusiastic support of my work.
This one's especially for you, Eamon, Nora, and Nellie!
—S.W.F.

Since 1888, the National Geographic Society has funded more than 12,000 research, exploration, and preservation projects around the world. The Society receives funds from National Geographic Partners, LLC, funded in part by your purchase. A portion of the proceeds from this book supports this vital work. To learn more, visit natgeo.com/info.

For more information, visit nationalgeographic.com, call 1-800-647-5463, or write to the following address:

National Geographic Partners
1145 17th Street N.W.
Washington, D.C. 20036-4688 U.S.A.

Visit us online at nationalgeographic.com/books

For librarians and teachers: ngchildrensbooks.org

More for kids from National Geographic:
natgeokids.com

National Geographic Kids magazine inspires children to explore their world with fun yet educational articles on animals, science, nature, and more. Using fresh storytelling and amazing photography, *Nat Geo Kids* shows kids ages 6 to 14 the fascinating truth about the world—and why they should care.
kids.nationalgeographic.com/subscribe

For information about special discounts for bulk purchases, please contact National Geographic Books Special Sales:
specialsales@natgeo.com

For rights or permissions inquiries, please contact National Geographic Books Subsidiary Rights:
bookrights@natgeo.com

Designed by Sanjida Rashid

Library of Congress Cataloging-in-Publication Data
Names: Flynn, Sarah Wassner, author.
Title: Know-it-all: ancient Egypt / by Sarah Wassner Flynn.
Other titles: Weird but true! (National Geographic Kids (Firm))
Description: Washington, DC: National Geographic Kids, 2019. | Series: Weird but true! | Includes index.
Identifiers: LCCN 2018035825| ISBN 9781426335457 (pbk.) | ISBN 9781426335464 (hardcover)
Subjects: LCSH: Egypt--Civilization--Juvenile literature.
Classification: LCC DT61 .F596 2019 | DDC 932--dc23
LC record available at https://lccn.loc.gov/2018035825

The publisher wishes to acknowledge everyone who helped make this book possible: Ariane Szu-Tu, editor; Sarah J. Mock and Danny Meldung, photo editors; Molly Reid, production editor; and Anne LeongSon and Gus Tello, design production assistants.

Printed in China
19/RRDS/1